The Remarkable Lives of 16 WWII Women Spies

Arianne Cousteau

© **Copyright 2021 - All rights reserved.**

The content contained within this book may not be reproduced, duplicated or transmitted without direct written permission from the author or the publisher.

Under no circumstances will any blame or legal responsibility be held against the publisher, or author, for any damages, reparation, or monetary loss due to the information contained within this book, either directly or indirectly.

Legal Notice:

This book is copyright protected. It is only for personal use. You cannot amend, distribute, sell, use, quote or paraphrase any part, or the content within this book, without the consent of the author or publisher.

Disclaimer Notice:

Please note the information contained within this document is for educational and entertainment purposes only. All effort has been executed to present accurate, up to date, reliable, complete information. No warranties of any kind are declared or implied. Readers acknowledge that the author is not engaged in the rendering of legal, financial, medical or professional advice. The content within this book has been derived from various sources. Please consult a licensed professional before attempting any techniques outlined in this book.

By reading this document, the reader agrees that under no circumstances is the author responsible for any losses, direct or indirect, that are incurred as a result of the use of the information contained within this document, including, but not limited to, errors, omissions, or inaccuracies.

Table of Contents

TABLE OF CONTENTS 5

INTRODUCTION: HEROISM OF WOMEN SPIES IN WWII 1
   WOMEN IN THE WAR EFFORT 1
   WOMEN AS SPIES AND OPERATIVES 2

CHAPTER 1: THE WILL TO FIGHT FASCISM 5
   WHAT IS A SPY? 5
   WHY TAKE THE RISK? 7
   MEDALS AND HONORS 8
      Croix de Guerre 8
      King's Commendation for Brave Conduct 8
      Légion d'Honneur 8
      Medaille de la Resistance 9
      Mentioned in Dispatches 9
      Most Excellent Order of the British Empire 9

CHAPTER 2: MARTHE HOFFNUNG COHN (APRIL 13, 1920 TO PRESENT) 11
   EARLY LIFE 11
   CAREER AS A SPY 13
   LIFE AFTER THE WAR 16

CHAPTER 3: JEANNIE YVONNE GHISLAINE ROUSSEAU (APRIL 1, 1919 TO AUGUST 23, 2017) 19
   EARLY LIFE 19
   CAREER AS A SPY 20
   LIFE AFTER THE WAR 24

CHAPTER 4: ODETTE SANSOM (APRIL 28, 1912 TO MARCH 13, 1995) 27
   EARLY LIFE 27
   CAREER AS A SPY 28
   LIFE AFTER THE WAR 32

CHAPTER 5: KRYSTYNA SKARBEK (MAY 1, 1908 TO JUNE 15, 1952) 33
   EARLY LIFE 33
   CAREER AS A SPY 34
   LIFE AFTER THE WAR 41

CHAPTER 6: VERA ATKINS (JUNE 16, 1908 TO JUNE 24, 2000) 43
- EARLY LIFE 43
- CAREER AS A SPY 44
- LIFE AFTER THE WAR 46

CHAPTER 7: ELAINE MARIE MADDEN (MAY 7, 1923 TO 2012) 49
- EARLY LIFE 49
- CAREER AS A SPY 51
- LIFE AFTER THE WAR 54

CHAPTER 8: BLANCHE CHARLET (MAY 23, 1898 TO OCTOBER 11, 1985) 57
- EARLY LIFE 57
- CAREER AS A SPY 58
- LIFE AFTER THE WAR 62

CHAPTER 9: MARGERY MYERS BOOTH STROHM (1906 TO APRIL 11, 1952) 63
- EARLY LIFE 63
- CAREER AS A SPY 65
- LIFE AFTER THE WAR 66

CHAPTER 10: NANCY GRACE AUGYSTA WAKE (AUGUST 13, 1912 TO AUGUST 7, 2011) 69
- EARLY LIFE 69
- CAREER AS A SPY 70
- LIFE AFTER THE WAR 73

CHAPTER 11: LISE DE BAISSAC (MAY 11, 1905 TO MARCH 29, 2004) 75
- EARLY LIFE 75
- CAREER AS A SPY 76
- LIFE AFTER THE WAR 80

CHAPTER 12: PHYLLIS LATOUR (APRIL 2, 1921 TO PRESENT) 81
- EARLY LIFE 81
- CAREER AS A SPY 82
- LIFE AFTER THE WAR 85

CHAPTER 13: MARY KATHERINE HERBERT (OCTOBER 1, 1903 TO JANUARY 23, 1983) 87
- EARLY LIFE 87
- CAREER AS A SPY 88
- LIFE AFTER THE WAR 92

CHAPTER 14: JOSEPHINE BAKER (JUNE 3, 1906 TO APRIL 12, 1975) 95

EARLY LIFE	95
CAREER AS A SPY	97
LIFE AFTER THE WAR	98

CHAPTER 15: ELIZABETH DEVEREUX-ROCHESTER (DECEMBER 20, 1917 TO MARCH 19, 1983) 101

EARLY LIFE	101
CAREER AS A SPY	102
LIFE AFTER THE WAR	105

CHAPTER 16: VIRGINIA HALL (APRIL 6, 1906 TO JULY 8, 1982) 107

EARLY LIFE	107
CAREER AS A SPY	108
LIFE AFTER THE WAR	114

CHAPTER 17: ELVIRA CHAUDOIR (1910/1911 TO JANUARY 1996) 117

EARLY LIFE	117
CAREER AS A SPY	118
LIFE AFTER THE WAR	121

BRAVERY OF REMARKABLE WOMEN 123

ABOUT THE AUTHOR 125

LIST OF ABBREVIATIONS 127

REFERENCES 129

Introduction:

Heroism of Women Spies in WWII

Women in the War Effort

World War II (WWII) left no one untouched. Everyone found themselves having to take up responsibilities that they had never previously considered. Women were no exception to this rule and played a substantial part in the war effort, both at home and on the front lines. At home, many women took up roles typically reserved for men, as so many able-bodied men were away on the front lines.

Many women found work in manufacturing. We all know the iconic Rosie the Riveter symbol in United States history. The manufacturing industry faced increasing demands due to the war effort and women stepped in to fill the need for workers. In 1943, women represented 65% of manufacturing workers, compared to just 1% in pre-war years (History.com Editors, 2010).

Some women joined the military, taking up administrative and clerical positions left behind by the increased need to deploy men to war zones and the front lines. To free up men to fight, these women continued to take on increased and varied tasks previously not open to women. These tasks included everything from performing vehicle maintenance and driving military cargo trucks, to piloting and delivering aircraft.

Many women served as nurses and nurses' aides tending injured soldiers. Still, other women wanted to take more direct action and took their fight to the enemy. The Allied forces were looking for a new way to disarm the enemy, and women spies were able to provide an answer that helped turn the tide of the intelligence arena.

Women as Spies and Operatives

The heroism of the women spies who chose to risk their lives is monumental. Many of them left behind families, husbands, children, parents, and siblings. But they knew the importance of the work. And they knew that battles were not just fought in the trenches with mechanical weaponry - they were also fought behind enemy lines, in cities and towns, in bars and bedrooms, and in the administrative offices of the opposing forces with information and secrets passing hands.

These women came from almost all Allied nations, and thus served different intelligence agencies and forces. In the United States, The Office of Strategic Services (OSS) offered a more centralized and direct way of coordinating intelligence. Eventually, the OSS had over 40 overseas offices. At its peak, women made up a large part of active operatives.

Women agents were especially active throughout the European and North African campaigns, and almost all Allied nations were represented. In particular, the United Kingdom's Secret Intelligence Service (MI6) and the organizations that comprised the French Resistance saw merit in employing female agents. Though spying was initially seen as a male-dominated endeavor, the French were among the first to challenge the idea that women were not suited for spy life and actively recruited women.

Eventually, women made up a quarter of United Kingdom's Special Operations Executive (SOE) ranks (Thomas & Lewis, 2017). British women and French nationals recruited to work for the SOE "F" Section honed new skills and steeled their resolve. The bravery of these women made a mark on the war efforts in ways that were not fully recognized and sometimes not fully known until after the war ended.

These women deserve to have their names and their stories remembered. Not just the stories of their grand adventures and courage during WWII, but also the stories of their childhoods and the journeys of espionage throughout the War, but also the rich lives they lived after the War ended. This book aims to provide a glimpse into some of WWII's most impressive and courageous spies.

o

Chapter 1:

The Will to Fight Fascism

What Is a Spy?

A spy in the context of WWII was someone who actively collected intelligence and plans of the enemy and brought them back to their respective agencies. They might also deliver false information to the enemy through deception to confuse their actions. Finally, they crossed into hostile territory to gather vital intelligence to benefit the Allied forces.

Being a spy meant crossing enemy lines and entering hazardous areas to collect vital information for the cause. During WWII, spies often served as couriers within the occupied territory who carried messages between Resistance circuits or transmitted intelligence back to London. Moving from place to place was frequently required to avoid detection.

The French Resistance was a collective of French anti-fascist organizations devoted to fighting the Nazi occupation of France and focused on disrupting Nazi supply lines and communications within France. The French Resistance was among the first to use women in their spy activities, and eventually, women made up a quarter of the of its ranks.

The British Secret Intelligence Service, MI6 played a major role in the information exchange among the Allied Forces, and its operations played a continual and crucial role in disrupting German operations. MI6 actively recruited women operatives and trained them to intercept German communications and feed misinformation back to the Nazis for the purpose of hampering German battle strategies and troop movements.

The British intelligence organization to employ many women spies was the Special Operations Executive (SOE). The SOE was created on July 22, 1940, to centralize several other British intelligence organizations and streamline communications with Allied intelligence organizations. Women served an important role as SOE operatives and could often pass through enemy checkpoints without attracting unwanted scrutiny.

The First Aid Nursing Yeomanry (FANY) was another British organization that aided the war effort and an agency that still exists. Formed in 1907, it was a nursing organization that eventually expanded services to work with the intelligence entities during World War I. At the onset of WWII, FANY was led by Mary Baxter Ellis, under whose leadership FANY worked closely with the SOE. FANY recruits undertook many roles outside of nursing, and many women were specially trained in wireless telegraphy and coding. This made them optimum candidates for espionage work. Of the 50 women sent into France by the SOE, 39 of them were members of FANY (Kramer, 1995).

In the United States of America, the Office of Strategic Services (OSS) was created to centralize intelligence efforts during wartime and monitor enemy activities in real time using the 1940s technology. To this goal, the OSS deployed spies and agents in various countries to have eyes and ears on the ground at all times. At its peak, the OSS had 40 overseas offices, and women made up a large part of their operation, both stateside and worldwide. Their information proved vital to the Allied forces. The OSS prevailed beyond the war effort, and it is the predecessor of the Central Intelligence Agency.

All of these agencies and organizations saw the benefit of having women among their ranks. The reason was simple: This was a time when women were more able to pass unnoticed. Rarely suspected of espionage or subterfuge, women could get in and out of tight spots without attracting too much attention. Seen as less threatening and less important by the male-dominated perceptions of the 1940s, women were able to move about more freely than their male counterparts.

Rather than being fit for the job despite not being men, women were recruited specifically because they could do jobs that men could not.

Women spies were recruited in various ways. Some were trusted individuals who were introduced to the right people. Others responded to requests for interviews with little knowledge of the details of what they would be doing. The common theme among these women is that they all said 'yes' when called upon.

The ages of the women described herein vary. The youngest was just a teenager when she began her work as a spy. It's hard to imagine someone so young deciding to take these risks, but at the time, these women knew what the mission called for. They gave everything they had to the worthiest of causes.

Why Take the Risk?

So why did so many people, including women, choose to risk their lives in this way? It was primarily due to a strong anti-fascist ideology. The aftershocks of World War I were still being felt by a vast portion of the British, European, and American populations when WWII began. Allied nations of the European theater knew that the only way to secure victory against the Nazi regime was to take direct and decisive action.

It is important to remember that the thirteen women described herein had lives before the war. They had families, fell in love, had hobbies and passions. They left so much behind when they joined the war effort. These women chose to be courageous in the fight against the fascist regime that threatened the world.

Medals and Honors

Due to the nature of bravery in the face of great danger, many of these women were awarded medals and honors. Some spies were recognized by more than one nation and received honors from each country. Whatever the distinction being bestowed, any one of them is something that deserves the utmost respect.

Croix de Guerre

Originating in 1915, the Croix de Guerre (war cross) honors those who fought with the Allies against the enemy and was typically reserved for those who served in military organizations.

King's Commendation for Brave Conduct

This honor, known as the Queen's Commendation for Brave Conduct during the reign of Queen Elizabeth II, was established in 1939. At the time of its inception and throughout WWII, the basis for eligibility was vague, making it an honor that could be bestowed upon non-combatants. Worthy acts of bravery by civilians or military personnel are recognized with this commendation.

Légion d'Honneur

Napoleon Bonaparte established this honor in 1802, making it one of the oldest honors bestowed for actions conducted during WWII. As time passed, the Légion d'Honneur became a medal given as the highest order of merit for military personnel and civilians. It is mainly given to French citizens, although there have been several historical exceptions.

Medaille de la Resistance

Established in 1943, this medal was a decoration bestowed by the French Committee of National Liberation during WWII. Rewarded both in life and posthumously, it was awarded to those who aided the French Resistance against the occupation. This medal was awarded not just to individuals, but to units, hospitals, and organizations as well.

George Cross

The George Cross was established in 1940 by King George VI to honor remarkable acts of civilian courage, particularly acts of courage displayed in the face of the enemy.

Mentioned in Dispatches

Although this honor does not come with a medal, it still carried weight. This honor meant that the soldier or operative's name was mentioned in an official written report by a superior officer and sent to high command, in which their courageous or meritorious action in the face of the enemy is described.

Most Excellent Order of the British Empire

The Most Excellent Order of the British Empire (MBE) is an order of chivalry. Established in June of 1917 by King George V, it comprises several civil and military categories. The two most senior divisions award a male the title "Sir" (knight) and a woman the title "Dame." Several of the women spies described herein were referred for this honor but were denied because the MBE cannot be bestowed posthumously.

Médaille Militaire

Established in 1852, this medal is considered the third highest award of the French Republic. It is a military decoration of the French Republic for other ranks for meritorious acts of bravery in action against enemy forces. During WWII, it reached a peak for the number of foreign designations, mostly to British and United States forces.

Chapter 2:

Marthe Hoffnung Cohn (April 13, 1920 to present)

Early Life

Marthe Hoffnung Cohn was born Marthe Cohn on April 13, 1920, in the French province of Lorraine to Orthodox Jewish parents. Though born before the peak of the war, Marthe later recalled that there still was anti-semitism taking place in Metz during her childhood in occupied France. Metz had been acquired by the Germans in 1871 as part of the Franco Prussian War and was only relinquished after World War I had ended. Because residents were not allowed to publicly speak French at the time of her birth, many citizens were basically German. That mandate did not exist by the time Marthe was born but she learned German in school, becoming fluent, something that would come in handy during her later missions. Although the town was no longer occupied during Marthe's formative years, bigotry remained, marring her childhood.

Marthe learned about hatred and what it cost those who were oppressed. When she was still growing up, she witnessed the aftermath of the defacement of the local synagogue, a clear message to the Jewish people in the area: 'You are not welcome.' It is no surprise that Cohn would see this world around her and eventually grow up wanting to do something about the injustice she saw.

When Hitler rose to power and trouble loomed on the horizon, Marthe and her family hid with other Mosellans at Poitiers in the department of Vienne in September of 1939. Following the French occupation in June of 1940, Marthe decided to stay in Vienne. Things changed dramatically for the family, bringing Marthe closer to her future path.

In June of 1942, Marthe's father and sister Stéphanie were arrested by the Gestapo and sent to prison. Her father was released shortly but her sister remained imprisoned for a month before eventually being transferred to a camp. Shaken by the event, Marthe organized an escape for her entire family to the free zone in southern France. She sent a message to her sister, hoping she might be able to escape and join them. , she received a response from Stéphanie that she was the only one providing medical assistance to imprisoned children. For this reason, she refused to attempt to join them. The family left without Stéphanie and Marthe was able to survive thanks to false papers that were put together before she left occupied territory. For the time being, she and most of her family were safe.

While in Poitiers, Marthe had met a man at a small get-together. After just that first meeting, the man—Jacques Delaunay—had decided he was going to marry Marthe. Flattered by his attention, Marthe danced with him all night and the two fell in love within weeks and were engaged to be married. She was 21 and she had found her great love.

The two were separated when Marthe's family fled occupied France. Still, the two stayed connected through letters and the occasional fleeting meet-up. Since Delauney was not Jewish and Marthe had her false papers, they were able to travel somewhat to meet whenever possible. In July of 1943, Delauney was in Paris and Marthe made the decision to meet him. It wasn't long before Marthe realized something was very wrong.

Delaunay, as it turned out, had been involved in Resistance work with his brother. During a sabotage scheme gone wrong, a Nazi collaborator had been fatally stabbed. He died of his injuries in a hospital, but not before he had told the authorities exactly what had transpired that night. Delaunay was in serious trouble.

Marthe was horrified at the news but wanted to keep her fiancé safe. She suggested he flee to Spain immediately to escape the inevitable repercussions. He refused, wanting to stay with his brother. So, Delaunay returned to his family to say farewell and collect his brother before making a go for Spain.

Delauney never made it to Spain. Marthe soon discovered that he and his colleagues had been arrested. She received no other news about Delaunay until the morning of October 25th, 1943. That morning, Marthe opened up the newspaper to find an article about five students from Poitiers. They were all sentenced to death, although one was spared and condemned to an indefinite term of imprisonment. Though she hoped that Delaunay was the one spared, she would later discover that he was among those executed. Marthe was devastated at the loss, but also driven.

Radicalized by her sister's imprisonment and her fiancé's untimely death, Marthe decided she had to do something about the horrors that were happening around her. With a new passion burning within her, she set her sights on pursuing a career that could change the course of the war that had ripped her family apart.

Career as a Spy

The month following the loss of her fiancé, Marthe finished up her studies at the nursing school of the French Red Cross in Marseilles. As soon as she was able, she tried to join the Resistance. , her efforts were in vain. Not to be deterred, she decided to seek other routes to help serve her country and the Allied Forces.

In November of 1944, after the liberation of Paris, Marthe enlisted with the French Army. When she first showed up for duty, she recalled later, her commander did not take her seriously as she had blonde hair and blue eyes. He took this observation to mean she had little substance (a view not uncommon at the time).

When beginning her career in intelligence, she initially offered her services as a nurse because that was her background. But there was no immediate need for nurses in their ranks. They did, however, have a need for a social worker. Marthe accepted the role but received very little direction on how to perform her duties. Because she was unsure how to carry out her role, she improvised by visiting French soldiers in the foxholes and bringing them supplies.

During one of her visits to the foxholes, Marthe encountered Colonel Pierre Fabien, a prominent figure in the French Resistance. He asked her if she would be willing to answer a phone call for him during a lunch break. She agreed to the task and followed him back to his home to complete it. While they were making conversation, Fabien discovered that Marthe was fluent in both German and French. This piqued his interest, and he asked her if should be willing to transfer to the Intelligence Service of the French 1st Army. Though unsure of the predicament she'd put herself in, she decided to accept the assignment.

In January of 1945, she was assigned to the Commanders d'Afrique near the Vosges Mountains in eastern France. The operation was overseen by Colonel Georges-Régis Bouvet, who assigned Marthe to interrogate German prisoners in order to gain information on the movement of their troops.

According to a later interview given by Marthe, she never tortured anyone for the information, however, she was able to provide very precise information to her superiors after interrogations, earning her several medals after the war ended. Impressed by her abilities, her superiors decided to make better use of her skills.

With the Allies advancing into Germany, Marthe was tasked with entering enemy territory to gain vital information. For her mission, she had been instructed to create her own cover story, as her superiors thought that it would make a more convincing cover than anything they could create for her. Marthe decided to pose as a German nurse from Alsace, searching for her missing fiancé.

Specifically, her mission in Germany was to spy on the activities of civilians in the town of Freiburg, and on soldiers at the nearby Siegfried

Line, a defensive line built alongside the German border. While on her way to the Siegfried Line, Marthe found herself in the company of Germans heading in the same direction. Due to her blonde hair, blue eyes, and fluency in German, they believed her well-constructed cover story. During her journey with the Germans, she met a schutzstaffel (SS, political soldiers of the Nazi party) officer who had taken ill. Being a good nurse, she cared for him. The man was grateful and asked her to visit him and gave her his phone number. At first, Marthe refused the offer, but she would reconsider in time.

Three weeks later, Marthe received word on the German radio that the Allies would be invading Freiburg. She rushed off to the Schutzstaffel (SS) Officer to obtain information. When she reached the Siegfried Line, she discovered there were very few troops there. It had been almost entirely evacuated. She hurried back to report the news to her superiors. By the time she arrived back at Freiburg, she found tanks waiting for her. The Allied invasion had already begun.

Marthe quickly realized something terrifying. Though her Aryan looks had served her well in infiltrating Germany, they now put her at danger if the Allied troops mistook her for a German and decided to kill her. Unsure what else to do, Marthe stood in the center of the street and held up Winston Churchill's V for victory sign. The tanks stopped in their approach and Marthe requested that the soldiers take her to the French headquarters as quickly as possible. When she arrived, she told her commander all about the abandoned Siegfried Line.

Her commander didn't believe her news at first, thinking it had to be an elaborate trap set by the Germans. He sent a patrol to the Line to confirm Marthe's story. They returned with the news that Line had, indeed, been completely evacuated. Marthe's intel was good.

The next morning, over breakfast, Marthe's commander asked her if she wanted to return to her work as a social worker for the organization. She rejected the idea, telling him that her mission ended on the day of armistice. She knew the importance of her work to the war effort, and she was not ready to relinquish the assignment.

The Allied forces prepared to continue their offensive into Germany. Marthe went ahead of them and came across a Nazi colonel. Sticking to her cover, she told him that she had fled from the French invasion of Freiburg and feigned distress over the German's plight. The German was sympathetic to the seemingly terrified Marthe and let her know that the war was not yet over, revealing to her that the remaining German forces were waiting to ambush in the Black Forest.

With this information, Marthe went immediately to Switzerland. There, she relayed the intelligence to the French Army. Because of her warning, they avoided the ambush and gained a tactical advantage that greatly contributed to their eventual victory against the Germans.

Highly regarded for her contributions to the intelligence work of the Allied Forces, Marthe has received several medals for her service. In 1945, she was awarded the Croix de Guerre, a medal that she remains very proud of to this day. More recently, she has received several honors that add to the prestige of this amazing spy's contributions. They include the Médaille militaire in 1999, the Medal of the Nation's Gratitude in 2002, and the Cross of the Order of Merit, Germany's highest honor.

Aside from the medals won, Marthe is also a member of two prestigious groups. She was dubbed a Knight in the Legion of Honor in 2002 and named a Woman of Valor by the Simon Wiesenthal Center that same year. At 101 years old, she is still a highly respected person of interest for her courageous and cunning actions during her career as a spy.

Life After the War

After the war, Marthe went on to build a family. Although she had lost her first true love to the horrors of WWII, she found love again, married, and had children. Still, she did not share her wartime activities with her children as she thought they'd find her tales ridiculous and unbelievable. Her children and grandchildren discovered her incredible contributions in 1999 when Marthe was awarded the Médaille Militaire.

Marthe is still alive, 101 years old, and is well respected for her contributions to the war effort. What she didn't expect was being awarded Germany's highest honor. She recalled in an interview how strange it was to her that she would one day be honored by the very country she fought against. The government felt that her actions had shortened the war, sparing further German lives. The president of the country invited Marthe over for tea with his wife in order to thank her for her actions.

Marthe remains an inspiration to many. Her courageous spirit and positive outlook have captured the hearts of people around the world. In 2002, she released an autobiography, focusing on her time working as a spy during WWII, entitled *Behind Enemy Lines: The True Story of a French Jewish Spy in Nazi Germany*. More recently, in 2019, she was the subject of a documentary, *The Accidental Spy*. The world has not forgotten her amazing accomplishments and still celebrates her today.

As for Marthe, she has words of wisdom for future generations: "Be engaged and do not accept any order that your conscience cannot approve of. These are the two [pieces of] advice I give children. If they follow this advice, they will be okay" (Burack, 2020).

Chapter 3:

Jeannie Yvonne Ghislaine Rousseau (April 1, 1919 to August 23, 2017)

Early Life

Jeannie Yvonne Ghislaine Rousseau was born on April 1, 1919, in Saint-Brieuc. Her parents were Jean Rousseau, a French foreign ministry official and World War I veteran, and his wife Marie. She grew up in relative comfort with a stable home life. Though a very public figure after the war, little has been published regarding Jeannie's childhood. There is no telling what personality she had as a child or what her early years held. As she grew older, it was clear Jeannie was well educated and taken care of, allowing her to grow into an intelligent and capable young woman.

She was a brilliant linguist who excelled in her studies at The Paris Institute of Political Studies (also called Sciences Po). Jeannie graduated with a degree in languages in 1939 from the University of Paris, right before the start of the war. It wasn't long before her expertise would be called for but for the time being, Jeannie still had a fire in her. She wanted to do something about the German occupation, no matter what that 'something' was.

After the outbreak of WWII, Jeannie moved with her family to Dinard, where her father hoped it would be safer. It was there she became an interpreter for the occupying German forces. Even before she was officially part of any intelligence organization, she began collecting intelligence on German operations. Her job at the French National Chamber of Commerce as an interpreter, and later as the organization's top staffer, put her in contact with German military command staff on a regular basis. She visited the Germans frequently, attempting to talk shop to get them to give up something valuable. She had no one to report her findings to. As Jeannie recalled later, "I was storing my nuts, but I had no way to pass them on" (Ignatius, 1998).

Jeannie would soon have her chance to pass on those 'nuts' of knowledge. It would be a while, and in the meantime, there was trouble on the horizon. She was starting to attract the wrong kind of attention. In 1941, she was arrested by the Gestapo on suspicion of spying. She was released not long after under the stipulation that she not live in the coastal area.

Career as a Spy

Later in 1941, Jeannie moved to Paris and shortly began working, again as an interpreter, for an association of French businessmen. She represented their interests and helped them negotiate contracts with the German occupiers. Beautiful and fluent in German, she quickly became a favorite among the German officers the association dealt with and by 1943, they trusted completely. They were also completely unaware that the woman they knew as "Madeleine Chauffeur" had been reporting to a French intelligence network organized by the Resistance.

Jeannie had actually begun her career as an official spy around the same time that she took the job as a translator in Paris. One night on a midnight train, she happened to run into an old friend and their conversation finally opened the door to real spy work. The old friend was Georges Lamarque, who remembered Jeannie from the University of Paris, where Jeannie had finished first in her class and had a special affinity for languages. Lamarque was a spy, working with the French Resistance and brought her into the fold of his network, the Druids.

In 1943, when Jeannie got wind of a secret weapons project, she endeavored to be on hand when the topic was discussed. She knew that she was in the position to overhear potential vital information without suspicion. When the topic was eventually discussed, Jeannie coaxed information out of the German officers through her natural charm. She feigned disbelief at the idea of the weapon, and it was convincing enough for one officer to show her drawings of the weapon in question, just to prove it to her. This secret weapons project would be revealed as the development of V2 and planned strikes.

Jeannie's reports were very well received by her superiors, who utilized the information to make strategic moves against the enemy. She continued to secretly pass intelligence on that so impressed the British intelligence analysts that they decided in the spring of 1944 to bring Jeannie to London for a debriefing. The pickup was planned for shortly after D-Day, an extraction of Jeannie and two other agents.

The extraction did not go to plan. The French agent who was supposed to lead them through the minefields was captured, blowing the operation. When Jeannie showed up at the rendezvous, the first to arrive, she bravely tried to warn the other agents. This allowed one to escape but the others were captured, along with Jeannie.

She was taken to the same Rennes prison where she had briefly been detained years earlier. At the time of her arrest, Jeannie was named in the newspapers as "Madeleine Chaufeur." Somehow, no one realized that she was the same woman arrested previously on suspicion of spying.

During her interrogation, Jeannie protested her innocence. She had been carrying two dozen pairs of French nylons, which she had planned to give as gifts to her British handlers. Thinking quickly, she wove a tale about planning to sell them on the black market in Brittany.

Despite her cover story, she was sent to a larger prison in Paris briefly before being transferred to the Ravensbrück concentration camp.

Jeannie arrived at Ravensbrück on August 15, 1944, her false papers that named her as Madeleine Chaufeur arriving after her, along with the evidence that she was part of an espionage ring. It was then that Jeannie played a clever trick on her captors. When asked for her name, she gave her real name, Jeannie Rousseau. Somehow, this ploy succeeded in confusing the Nazis, who were never able to match the prisoner with her spy identity.

The concentration camp, predictably, was a dismal place and most of the prisoners had all but lost hope by the time Jeannie arrived. She decided that it was the responsibility of the new arrivals to uplift those who had been there a while. Jeannie was able to keep up her hopeful attitude because she knew that D-Day had happened. She knew that the Allies were making incredible strides and believed liberation would be right around the corner.

During her time in the camps, Jeannie resolved that she did not want to do anything that would aid the Germans in the war. She made a pact with two French women in the camp with her that they would not do any work that would support the German war machine. True to their word, when the women were transferred to the sub-camp of Torgau to work at a munitions facility, the women refused to take part in the work. In fact, she staged a protest. She approached the chief of the camp and gave a speech in fluent German. The women were prisoners of war (POWs) and, under the Geneva convention, the Gestapo had no right to force them to make ammunition. It was a risky gamble, but it somehow paid off by lifting the spirits of the other prisoners, just as Jeannie had wanted.

Her stunt was not without its consequences. Following her protest, she was sent back to Ravensbrück proper for interrogation. There was still confusion about her identity as "Jeannie" did not exist in their documents. When she was asked by the interrogators why she had been sent to the camp, Jeannie played dumb and acted like she had no idea. Despite this confusion, the Gestapo still knew that this woman was a troublemaker. She and the other two instigators were sent to the punishment camp of Konigsberg.

Konigsberg was a dreadful and hopeless place, much worse than the conditions Jeannie had experienced in Ravensbrück. As part of their punishment, the women were forced into brutal manual labor, hauling rocks and gravel to build an airstrip. After a long day hard at work, the women would line up for their evening meal of hot soup. The head guard often enjoyed tipping the vat of soup over and watching the desperate prisoners scramble for their food.

Despite these conditions, Jeannie managed to keep her fighting spirit. She concluded that the prisoners' chance of survival would drastically improve if those outside knew that the prisoners were alive. She tasked herself with conducting a census of the camp, collecting names of over 400 women on tiny slips of paper that were eventually passed through the barbed wire to French POWs being held at a neighboring camp. Astoundingly, the POWs were somehow able to get the names to the Red Cross in Switzerland.

Meanwhile, Jeannie's health was quickly deteriorating. The brutal manual labor and cruel treatment were taking a toll on her body. She knew that escape was necessary if she were to survive. In desperation and determination, Jeannie came up with a truly bizarre escape plan.

At the time of Jeannie's crazy plan, there was an outbreak of typhoid and several of the women at the camp had contracted it. There was a truck coming to pick them up to transport them to the gas chambers of Ravensbrück. Jeannie and her two friends snuck onto the truck with the rest of the women. The trip took nearly 2 days and there was no food. When the truck finally arrived at Ravensbrück, it paused for a few moments before heading toward the gas chambers. In those brief moments, Jeannie and her friends snuck out of the truck and slipped back into the camp, unnoticed. Their plan, as it stood, was to blend back into Ravensbrück.

Needing help desperately, the women immediately went to the French barracks in search of help. Without prisoner numbers, they had no access to the shelter or little food the camp offered. They needed allies.

When they arrived at the barracks, their French compatriots agreed to help them for one day only. Following their short stay there, the three women made their way to the Polish barracks, where they were sheltered for several days. Eventually, it seemed their luck had run out. An informer tipped off the Gestapo to their presence and the three were taken to the Ravensbrück inner prison, where they were treated cruelly.

She was kept on half rations and made to do manual labor again. Her health, again, began to deteriorate and Jeannie feared the worst.

Eventually, after having been blocked from rescue once, Jeannie was rescued by the Swedish Red Cross. Knowing her name would probably be on their list, she decided her last chance was to intimidate the guard holding her. She began screaming and acting wild at the guard, frightening the woman. Terrified, the woman handed Jeannie and her two friends over to the Red Cross. They had succeeded in escaping at last.

Life After the War

Due to her poor health at the time of her rescue, Jeannie received surgery and spent time recuperating at a sanitarium in France. It was there that she met Henri de Clarens, a man who had survived Buchenwald and Auschwitz. The two fell in love and eventually married, having two children together.

Jeannie received several coveted honors immediately following her service. She was awarded the Resistance Medal and the Croix de Guerre in honor of her courageous work. She would receive more honors in her lifetime, but for now she had these medals as reminders of the great work she had accomplished and the tenacity she had to survive.

After the war, Jeannie's linguistic talents were still in high demand. She continued to work as an interpreter, this time, for agencies such as the

United Nations. In 1955 she was awarded the Légion d'honneur. For decades after the war, Jeannie continued her work and kept her fascinating tale of intrigue to herself. Her story was left untold for far too long.

, that all changed in 1998 when she finally gave an interview on her wartime experiences. Audiences responded well to the article, and she began to give more interviews and even did several talks about her life. The world began to recognize Jeannie for the extraordinary woman that she was. In 2009, Jeannie's previous Légion d'honneur medal was supplemented by the Grand Officer medal.

Jeannie went on to live a long and happy life following the war. This woman, so determined to pursue dangerous intelligence work, managed to aid the Allied Forces. She had helped turn the tide of the war. But most of all, she had survived. She had faced insurmountable odds and she had survived. Her incredible courage and inability to give up make her one of the most inspirational women in history. When she died in 2017 at the age of 98, she left behind an inspiring legacy of courage and hope.

Chapter 4:

Odette Sansom (April 28, 1912 to March 13, 1995)

Early Life

Odette Sansom was born Odette Brailly on April 28, 1912, in Amiens, France. Her mother was Emma and her father, Florentin Brailly, a bank manager. Though she was born into a well-off family, Odette suffered much in her early years. When she was still a young child, her father, who was serving with the French Army, was killed at Verdun shortly before the Armistice in 1918. Though he was posthumously awarded honors for his service, Odette was still a girl now growing up without a father.

Furthermore, Odette was not a healthy child. When young, she contracted serious illnesses that left her blind for over 3 years. She also contracted polio, leaving her bedridden for months. During her childhood, she was convent-educated, and the staff often described her as difficult, though historians theorize this may have been due to her many illnesses. It might seem unusual that a girl with such delicate health would grow up to be the woman who worked as a spy in German-occupied territories.

Despite the difficulties she faced in childhood, Odette grew up to be a beautiful and capable young woman. In 1931, she married a hotel worker named Roy Sansom. Together, the couple moved to London and had three daughters: Françoise Edith, Lili, and Marianne. Odette, at first, was content with her role as a mother and housewife, but the war would change all that. The war completely altered Odette's world, much as it had done for millions of others.

Career as a Spy

At the beginning of WWII, Odette's husband joined the army. For safety, Odette and the children moved to Somerset in the south of France. They lived there in relative quiet for a few years until a bizarre mail mix-up would bring Odette to the attention of the SOE. It was spring of 1942, and the Admiralty appealed for postcards or family photographs taken on the coast for possible war use. Odette heard the broadcast announcing the appeal and wrote a letter stating that she had photographs taken around Boulogne. She mistakenly sent the letter to the War Office instead of the Admiralty.

This simple, mistakenly sent letter ended up in the hands of the SOE, bringing Odette to their attention. She was recruited shortly thereafter and enlisted in FANY as a cover for her secret work, one of the first SOE agents to be brought into the organization. Answering the call to aid the war effort, Odette reluctantly dropped her three daughters off at a convent school and left for London, where she would begin training to be an intelligence operative.

She knew that they intended to send her into occupied territory. She knew the risk, and that she might never see her daughters again. Still, Odette knew the importance of the cause and chose to aid it anyway. She wanted to help her home country and was willing to sacrifice to be part of the fight to protect it.

Originally, Odette was not thought to be great spy material. She was considered too temperamental and stubborn by her superiors in the SOE. An early report even stated: "She is impulsive and hasty in her judgments and has not quite the clarity of mind which is desirable in subversive activity. She seems to have little experience of the outside world. She is excitable and temperamental, although she has a certain determination" (Escott, 2012). This was not exactly a glowing recommendation of Odette's accountability in the field. The SOE also noted that she was passionate about doing what she could to help France. Maurice Buckmaster, leader of the SOE, allowed Odette to continue on.

On November 2, 1942, she landed on a beach near Cassis and contacted Captain Peter Churchill, Winston Churchill's nephew and the head of Spindle. Spindle was an SOE network that operated out of Cannes. Within the group, Odette's codename was "Lise" and her main objective was to contact the French Resistance and set up a safehouse for other operatives. Odette arrived at a time of strife for the Spindle network.

Due to a misplaced list of potential supporters, the network had just lost their courier and Odette was stranded in Cannes. Obtaining Buckmaster's permission to change Odette's mission, Churchill made Odette the new courier for the network. Suddenly, instead of setting up a safehouse, she was required to find food and lodging for Adolphe Rabinovitch, the network's radio operator. In France illegally, Rabinovitch had no ration card.

She was also responsible for tending to air drops that occasionally ended in dangerous areas by accident. Her work within the network initially brought her to Marseilles, which was considered a dangerous town due to its infiltration by German agents. The danger had never been more real for Odette, and she was beginning to realize how lax the security was with the network. She grew close with Churchill and Rabinovitch but began to suspect that there was disloyalty within the group. She declined, in later interviews, to divulge whom she suspected.

Odette was not the only one who sensed trouble on the horizon. In January of 1943, Peter Churchill and Rabinovitch traveled with Odette north of the Riviera to the French Alps, as they were feeling vulnerable to German capture. Odette and Churchill took up residence at a hotel in the village of Saint-Jorioz. They were joined there by members of the Carte network, which unfortunately drew the attention of the

Gestapo. In early spring of 1943, an SOE agent assessed the security of Churchill's team to be deficient. It was his belief that they were leaving themselves open to capture.

While Odette and Churchill's team resided in Saint-Jorioz, trouble was brewing in Paris. It was there, in mid-March, that spy-catcher Hugo Bleicher of German counterintelligence arrested a network operative. He was successful in convincing this agent and his colleague that he was actually an anti-Nazi colonel. He suggested they work together, and the two agents readily agreed, convinced of his cover story. From the agents, Bleicher received the location of the network and a letter of introduction to the unsuspecting agents. He proceeded to the hotel where the agents resided and introduced himself as "Colonel Henri."

After Bleicher departed the hotel, Odette had Rabinovitch send a wireless message to SOE headquarters in London, reporting the contact with his new character. The response from London was immediate: "Henri highly dangerous...you are to hide across lake and cut contacts with all save [Rabinovitch]" (Loftis, 2019).

At the time of the unfortunate meeting, Churchill was in London consulting with the SOE. He was warned at the time to avoid any contact with Odette and Colonel Henri when he returned to France. To his surprise, , when he parachuted back into France on April 15th, he was met by Odette and Rabinovitch. Given the fact that Odette did not expect the return of Colonel Henri until the 18th, she returned with Churchill to the hotel. In the early morning of April 16th, Bleicher returned to the hotel with Italian soldiers and had them arrested, no longer under the cover of "Colonel Henri."

Odette was interrogated and tortured on numerous occasions at Fresnes Prison in the early days of her imprisonment. The torture was extreme and especially cruel but even under that pressure, Odette remained steadfast in her concocted story: that she - not Churchill - was the leader. Churchill, Winston Churchill's nephew, was just her husband and unaware of her activities. She also refused to give any information on other members.

During her imprisonment, the double agent who had betrayed her—whom she now knew was Bleicher—would visit her and invite her on trips to Paris with him. Odette was not one to be swayed by this tactic either and refused these overtures. Finally, the Nazis grew tired of attempting to break her and she was sentenced to death on two counts in June of 1943. Upon hearing this, Odette said: "Then you will have to make up your mind on what count I am to be executed, because I can only die once" (Starns, 2018). Angered by her insolence, Bleicher had her sent to Ravensbrück concentration camp.

Upon arriving at the Ravensbrück, Odette was kept in a punishment block and kept on a starvation diet. From her cell, she could hear the sounds of other prisoners being beaten. These already bad conditions worsened after the Allied landings in the south of France in August of 1944. On orders from Berlin, all food was withdrawn for a week, the lights were cut out in Odette's cell, and the heat was turned up.

The doctors of the camp argued that there was no way that Odette would survive the conditions in her cell. Although she was found unconscious, she survived and was put in solitary confinement. When she was eventually moved to the ground floor that December, the conditions greatly improved for Odette. The cell was still near a crematorium and ash from the executions would sometimes settle on Odette in her cell.

Eventually, Odette was released. The camp commandant, Fritz Suhren, took her from her cell and drove to a nearby American base to surrender. Having believed Odette's earlier story, he hoped her supposed connections to Winston Churchill would allow him to negotiate his way out of an execution. Thanks to her quick thinking under pressure, she was finally free.

Life After the War

After the war, Odette returned to her husband and children. Something had changed in the time that she was away and ultimately, the marriage dissolved in 1946. The same year, she testified in the Hamburg–Ravensbrück Trials against the prison guards charged with war crimes. Perhaps it was the fact that she had come back from the war a changed woman that caused the marriage to fail. It's possible, though, there were other factors. The very next year, she married her SOE partner, Peter Churchill.

For her service, Odette was awarded many honors. Her quick thinking saved her life and probably that of Churchill. The French government honored her with the Légion d'honneur for her service to the country she wanted to protect so fiercely. The United Kingdom also saw fit to award her with several medals and honors, including the George Cross, the 1939–1945 Star, the Defense Medal, and the War Medal 1939–1945.

She was honored with an adaptation of her wartime efforts in a 1950 film, entitled *Odette*. Odette, then known as Odette Churchill, wrote a personal message that appeared at the end of the movie. The film was well received.

By 1955, Odette and Churchill had divorced. Odette went on to marry Geoffrey Hallowes, another fellow SOE agent, in 1956. She remained married to Hallowes until March 13, 1995, when she passed away at the age of 82.

Her death did not end her wartime legacy. Still a celebrated figure, Odette was honored in several ways posthumously. In 2012, the Royal Mail released a postage stamp featuring Odette as part of its "Britons of Distinction" series. In 2019, a biography of Odette's life was released under the title *Code Name: Lise*. The world has not yet forgotten the sacrifices that this incredible woman made to keep her country free.

Chapter 5:

Krystyna Skarbek (May 1, 1908 to June 15, 1952)

Early Life

Krystyna was born on May 1, 1908, in Warsaw, Poland to Count Jerzy Skarbek and his wife Stefania, the daughter of a wealthy assimilated Jewish family. Count Jerzy found himself in a fortuitous marriage and immediately used his wife's sizable dowry to pay off his debts and continue living his lavish lifestyle. The couple's first child, Andrzej, took after the mother's side of the family, while Krystyna took after her father and inherited his love for riding horses.

While riding horses was one of her favorite hobbies, she also enjoyed other activities, at which she often excelled. She became an expert skier during family visits to Zakopane in the mountains of southern Poland. Krystyna was a true tomboy, and due to this fact, she shared a close rapport with her father, who greatly approved of her pursuits.

Charismatic and incredibly talented, she was most likely expected to take her place in aristocratic society after she completed her education. , that fate was not in the cards for Krystyna, whose father financially ruined the family with his decadent lifestyle. When he died in 1930, he left them in near poverty.

That same year, Krystyna had a whirlwind romance with Gustaw Gettlich and the two were soon married. The union did not last. The couple ultimately proved to be incompatible, and they quickly divorced. She pursued a subsequent love affair, but it was quickly shut down by the man's disapproving mother, who refused to consider a penniless divorcee as a daughter-in-law.

Krystyna, not wanting to be a burden to her widowed mother, began working at a Fiat car dealership. She soon became ill from the automobile fumes and had to leave the position. The fumes had done damage to her lungs and on medical advice, Krystyna left for a skiing trip in the clean air of the Tatra mountains, funding it with compensation benefits she received from her former employer.

It was on the slopes of these mountains that she met her second husband. Krystyna lost control on her skis one day and was rescued by a giant of a man who stepped into her path to stop her descent. Her rescuer was Jerzy Giżycki, a brilliant but moody eccentric who came from a wealthy family. He told her of his adventurous life: how he had left home at 14 after a fight with his father and worked as a cowboy and gold prospector in the United States, and how he eventually became a writer who traveled in search of inspiration for his work. She fell for him and the two were married in November of 1938. Shortly after, Giżycki took a post in Ethiopia and the couple moved there together.

Career as a Spy

At the outbreak of WWII, Krystyna sailed with her husband to London. Once there, she sought to offer her services in the fight against the fascist regime that threatened the world. At first, British authorities showed very little interest in employing Krystyna, but they were eventually convinced by her acquaintances, who introduced her to the Secret Intelligence Service (SIS, also known as MI6). She was first mentioned by the SIS in December of 1939, where she was described as a "flaming Polish patriot, expert skier, and great adventuress"

(Mulley, 2014). They also noted her apparent fearlessness, which greatly impressed them.

Now a British agent, Krystyna left London for Budapest, Hungary, arriving on December 21, 1939. Though Hungary was not yet a participant in the war, their allegiance was leaning towards Germany. She slipped into the country with the cover of being a journalist. Upon her arrival, Krystyna persuaded Polish Olympic skier Jan Marusarz to escort her across the Tatra Mountains into German-occupied Poland to see her mother.

When Krystyna arrived, she begged her mother to flee to safety. Stefania, , refused her daughter's request and opted to stay in Warsaw, where she was teaching French to young children. Much to Krystyna's dismay, she would not be swayed, and she remained in Poland, was arrested in 1942, and disappeared into Warsaw's Pawiak Prison.

Krystyna had no choice but to leave her mother behind and go to Hungary, where she was initially meant to go. While there, she encountered Andrzej Kowerski, whom she had briefly met when they were both children. He was now a Polish army officer. Due to a pre-war hunting injury, Kowerski had lost part of his leg and was now exfiltrating Allied military personnel and collecting intelligence. Krystyna helped organize a network of Polish couriers who would bring intelligence from Warsaw to Budapest.

At MI6's request, she and Kowerski began organizing surveillance of all rails, river, and road traffic on the borders with Romania and Germany. Krystyna is credited, during this time, with providing intelligence on oil transports to Germany from Romania's Ploiesti oil fields, a report that proved extremely useful to the analysts that received it. It gave the Allies a significant advantage.

Krystyna spent much of 1940 going back and forth between Poland and Hungary, continuing her tasks. Trouble came for them in January of 1941, when she and Kowerski were arrested by the Hungarian police. They were imprisoned and interrogated by the Gestapo until Krystyna feigned the symptoms of pulmonary tuberculosis. She bit her tongue until it bled, leading a doctor to incorrectly diagnose her with the disease. The Germans decided to release them, but the couple was followed by the police afterwards. Knowing now that Hungary was a strong German ally, the couple decided to flee the country.

It was the British Ambassador in Hungary, Owen O'Malley, and his novelist wife Ann Bridge, who helped Krystyna and Kowerski escape Hungary. O'Malley issued fake passports to each of them. Kowerski became "Anthony Kennedy" while Krystyna received the name "Christine Granville." She would go on to use this name for the rest of her life. Krystyna was smuggled out of Hungary in the trunk of O'Malley's Chrysler by a British Embassy driver, while Kowerski drove his own car across the border.

The two reunited later in Yugoslavia and were met by O'Malley when they reached Belgrade. They enjoyed a short reprieve before Kowerski and Krystyna continued on their mission, their first stop being Sofia, Bulgaria, where they met up with air attache Aidan Crawley. They passed microfilm along to him that they had received from a Polish intelligence organization known as the Musketeers. The microfilm contained photographs of a Germany military buildup near their border with the Soviet Union, indicating that the Germans planned to invade the Soviet Union.

The microfilm was considered so important that it was sent to Winston Churchill himself, who was stunned by the contents. , by March, Churchill was convinced of the legitimacy of the intelligence when he received information from other sources that confirmed it. The Germans invaded the Soviet Union in June of 1941.

Krystyna and Kowerski left Bulgaria and continued on to Istanbul, Turkey, where they tried to ensure the continuing functionality of the courier routes from Istanbul to Poland. Krystyna's husband met the pair there in March of 1941. They managed to persuade him to take up Krystyna's former role as the contact point for the British with the Polish Resistance. The pair continued their journey through Syria and Lebanon, until they reached Cairo in May of 1941.

When they arrived at the SOE offices, Krystyna learned that she was under suspicion because of her contact with the Mustketeers organization and the ease with which she was able to secure transit visas throughout their travels in hostile territories. Some of the SOE agents believed that only German spies could have secured those visas. They were summarily dismissed by SOE agent Peter Wilkinson when he arrived in Cairo in June.

They were kept on the SOE payroll, however, on a pithy retainer that had them living in near poverty. Eventually, Kowerski, who was under less suspicion than Krystyna, was able to resume his intelligence work by clearing up misunderstandings with General Kopański. Krystyna was still under suspicion.

When Krystyna's husband discovered that she had been dismissed from the SOE, he abruptly left his career as an intelligence officer with the organization in protest. He was about to receive devastating news from his wife. Krystyna admitted that, during their time working together, she had fallen in love with Kowerski. Crestfallen, her husband left for London, eventually emigrating to Canada. (Their marriage would be dissolved after the war.)

Until 1943, Krystyna was relegated to small tasks by the SOE, such as intelligence gathering in Cairo and Syria. She would occasionally pass information along to the British on Polish intelligence agencies. She was also offered office work, but she steadfastly refused. She was becoming bitter at being sidelined from the dangerous missions she had signed up for. Throughout it all, Krystyna remained under suspicion, much to her frustration.

Eventually, she found a road back to the SOE and it started with joining FANY. The SOE officer who reinstated her later joked, "The most useful thing I did in World War II was to reinstate Christine Granville" (Mulley, 2014). She made a good impression on her FANY superiors and was quickly reinstated for work. Despite her experience in clandestine work, she was given training for prospective agents. She proved to be greatly lacking in wireless transmitting and firearms, but excelled in parachuting, which she grew to love.

Eventually, the SOE was satisfied, and Krystyna was scheduled to infiltrate southern France. She parachuted into the territory on the night of July 7th, 1944, where she made contact and began working with the Jockey network, headed by Francis Cammaertes. The job Cammaertes and his team were tasked with was organizing the French Resistance fighters in southeastern France to weaken the German occupiers. Krystyna served as courier for Cammaertes and was also given the task of attempting to subvert the Polish conscripts in the German army, stationed along the Franco–Italian border.

Krystyna's arrival coincided with a large operation headed by British major, Desmond Longe, of supplying the local Maquis (French Resistance fighters) with arms and supplies via parachute. Krystyna, finally back to the missions she wanted, was out every night, organizing a reception committee to collect the canisters dropped by Allied airplanes.

The morning of July 14 spelled trouble for the network. That day there was to be a daylight drop of arms and supplies, the biggest drop yet to the Maquis. Encouraged by the supplies and a speech given by the head of the provisional government, a full-scale rebellion broke out against the German occupiers, much to Cammaertes's dismay. The strike turned out to be premature and was easily crushed by the German troops. A week later and under fire, Krystyna and Cammaertes fled the area, setting up a new base at Seynes-les-Alpes.

Once having escaped, Krystyna embarked on a 3-week journey, mostly on foot, through the Alps. She carried a rucksack with her at all times, filled with food and hand grenades. On her journey, she contacted prominent leaders of the French Resistance—Gilbert Galletti and Paul Hérault—and welcomed the arrival of the Operation Toplink team, which included several of her friends.

The purpose of the operation was to organize and supply the French and Italian Resistance along the border. After some time working on the operation, Krystyna took on a great risk, hoping that the rewards would be worth it. She approached a formidable fortress, manned by 150 Polish soldiers, and revealed her true identity in Polish. She spoke with dozens of Polish soldiers and instructed them to destroy and abandon the fortress when the order was given by the Resistance forces.

A little less than a week later, a small force of two Maquis officers of Operation Toplink approached the garrison. The German commander surrendered the fortress and gave up his mutinous soldiers. The Poles present in the garrison joined the French Resistance as Krystyna had instructed.

While this was occurring, Cammaertes had run into trouble. On August 13, 1944, he was arrested at a roadblock with two of his colleagues. Deeply troubled by the news, Krystyna rushed back, stopping briefly along her way to greet a recently arrived 10-man allied military mission. She told them that she was in charge in Cammaertes's absence and arranged transportation for them. Subsequently, she attempted to persuade French Resistance leaders to storm the prison where Cammaertes was being held, without success. Frustrated with her inaction, she traveled 25 miles by bicycle to Digne, where Cammaertes was being held.

She arrived at Digne on August 15th and circled the walls of the prison, humming "Frankie and Johnny," a favorite tune of hers and Cammaertes. He hummed the tune back, confirming that he was inside. Determined to rescue him, Krystyna came up with a plan to get him out.

Krystyna managed to meet with Captain Albert Schnenck, a liaison officer between the local French prefecture and the Gestapo. Desperate to get Cammaertes freed, she introduced herself as Cammaertes's wife and niece of British General Bernard Montgomery. Using her fabricated connections, Krystyna threatened Schnenck with terrible retribution if any harm came to the prisoners. She reinforced her threat with a bribe, an offer of two million francs for the men's release.

Following Krystyna's risky plan, she contacted the SOE in London about her offer and the money was shortly airdropped to her. She returned to the prison on August 17th with the money in hand. Shnenck ushered her in and introduced her to Max Waem, a Belgian with the authority to release the prisoners.

At her meeting with him, Krystyna bargained with Waem, turning the full force of her magnetic personality on him. Krystyna explained that the Allies would be arriving at any moment and she, a British parachutist, was in near constant contact with the British forces. She was convincing enough that Waem was willing to hear her out. He placed his gun on the table between them and asked her what she would do to protect him if he released the prisoners.

Persuaded to do as Krystyna said, Waem marched the prisoners out of the prison later that evening, all dressed in SS uniforms to avoid suspicion. He drove them to the outskirts of Digne where Krystyna was awaiting their arrival. There, they buried the SS uniforms, and the men were freed.

The American army liberated the prison 2 days later as part of Operation Dragoon. On August 20th, Krystyna and Cammaertes offered their help to the American commander, Frederic B. Butler, but he dismissed them as common bandits. Krystyna had little care for rank and was furious at his response, having to be calmed down by the general's aid.

Departing, the two proceeded to Gap, where the Germans had been captured by the Maquis. Among the captured Germans were several hundred Poles. Krystyna addressed them through a megaphone and secured their agreement to join the Allied forces, as long as they got rid of their German uniforms. The Poles were persuaded by Krystyna, and all stripped off their German uniforms in order to join the Allied forces. They could sense the tide of the war was changing. From there, the pair continued to Lyon and Paris, Krystyna eventually leaving for London in September.

Krystyna and Kowerski were cleared of suspicion and reconciled with the Polish forces by this point. By early 1945, Krystyna and Kowerski were preparing to drop into Poland, however, the mission was canceled because the first company to land in Poland had been immediately captured by the Red Army. By the end of the war, Krystyna had transferred to the Women's Auxiliary Air Force (WAAF) as a flight officer until the end of the war in Europe.

Krystyna's fierce determination and quick thinking served the war effort well. She undoubtedly gave the Allies an advantage on multiple occasions. Her service was greatly recognized, and she received several awards and honors for her time of service, including the George Medal, the France and Germany Star, the War Medal, the Croix de Guerre, and the Italy Star. Furthermore, she was made an Officer of the Order of the British Empire.

Life After the War

After the war, Krystyna found herself in a difficult position. She was left without any financial reserves or a native country to return to. Unable to find work following her service, she traveled to Nairobi to join Michael Dunford, an old lover. The government turned down her application for a work permit. Suddenly, a woman who had done so much for the world was being denied a way to make a living.

She returned to London where she worked various jobs, including a telephone operator, waitress, and a cabin steward on ocean liners. On one of the ocean liners where she worked, the crew were required to wear any medals awarded during the war. Krystyna's impressive number of medals and ribbons made her a favorite among the passengers but an object of resentment among the rest of the crew.

Unfortunately, Krystyna did not live long after the war. In June of 1952, she was stabbed to death in a London hotel. She had booked into the hotel on June 14th after returning from a voyage on which she had served as a steward. Her attacker was Dennis Muldowney, a man who had become obsessed with Krystyna while they worked together on an ocean liner.

Following her death, a group of men including Cammaertes and the two other prisoners she'd freed were determined to uphold her good name. They dedicated themselves to making sure her name would not be sullied in the wake of her death. Long after their deaths, the hotel at which Krystyna had died announced it would place a blue plaque for her in 2020. It was unveiled in September; Krystyna having left her mark on the world in more ways than one.

She had done her best to turn the tide of the war. Her contributions were not forgotten, despite her early death. Despite being underestimated and the object of suspicion throughout her career, Krystyna proved everyone wrong and was a valuable asset to the Allied forces, leaving behind an incredible legacy.

Chapter 6:

Vera Atkins (June 16, 1908 to June 24, 2000)

Early Life

Easily one of the most controversial spies in this book, Vera Atkins was born Vera May Rosenberg in Romania to parents German–Jewish Max Rosenberg and his British–Jewish wife Zefra Hilda, known as Hilda. Vera grew up with her parents and two brothers in Galati, Romania.

Unfortunately, Vera's father went bankrupt in 1932 and died just a year later. In the wake of his death, Vera remained with her mother in Romania until eventually emigrating to Britain in 1937. The abrupt move was in response to the threatening political situation happening in Europe. Around this time, Vera met a young British pilot named Dick Ketton-Cremer and the two were briefly engaged. Sadly, Ketton-Cremer was killed during the Battle of Crete in 1941. Vera never married after that. She and her mother returned to Europe, and she continued living with her mother in their flat throughout her time in the SOE and until her mother's death after the war.

Vera was well educated but somewhat flighty in her pursuits. She briefly studied modern languages at the Sorbonne in Paris for modern languages before heading to a finishing school at Lausanne, where she indulged her passion for skiing. Much like Krystyna Skarbek, she had a natural affinity for sport. When she was living in England, she enrolled in a secretary training school in London.

While living in Romania, Vera brushed shoulders with several notable diplomats who were members of British intelligence. Not only would these men eventually launch her spy work career, but they would also help her obtain her British citizenship down the line. It is possible during this time that, due to Vera's pro-British views, she also might have provided them with information as a 'stringer.' During this time Vera also worked as a translator and representative for an oil company.

In the spring of 1940, Vera was desperate to help her cousin Fritz escape Romania. She traveled to the Low Countries to bribe an Abwehr (German military intelligence service) officer for a passport to give Fritz. When the Germans invaded on May 10, 1940, Vera found herself stranded in The Netherlands. After going into hiding to escape detection, she was able to return to England in late 1940 with the assistance of a Belgian escape network. Before she began her work with the SOE, she initially volunteered her services as an Air Raid Precautions warden.

Career as a Spy

Not long after her return to England, Vera was recruited by Canadian spymaster William Stephenson, who worked for the British Security Coordination. Seeing her potential and drive, he sent her on fact-finding missions across Europe to supply Winston Churchill with intel on the rising threat that Nazi posed.

Despite not being a British national, Vera became involved with the French Section (otherwise known as "F" Section) of the SOE in February of 1941. Originally, she served as a secretary within the SOE, possibly due to her experience in secretarial school. She proved herself to be too valuable for simple clerical work. Eventually, she became one of the most vital women in the organization.

Vera was eventually made the assistant. Though not technically a spy, Vera's work within the organization was vital to the intelligence work being done to aid the war effort. She was made assistant to section head Maurice Buckmaster, becoming a de facto intelligence officer. Vera served as a civilian until 1941, when she was eventually commissioned a Flight Officer in the WAAF, having been naturalized as a British subject earlier that year. She was later appointed "F" Section's intelligence officer.

During her time with the SOE, Vera's primary role was the recruitment and deployment of British agents in occupied France. She would bring new agents into the fold and get them ready for their missions across enemy lines. An invaluable service, her story is intertwined with the stories of so many women in this book and the previous volume.

Aside from recruitment, Vera was responsible for the 37 female SOE agents working as couriers and wireless operators for the various SOE-established networks. She would attend to any 'housekeeping' related to the agents under her care. She would check their clothing and paperwork before sending them out on a mission to ensure that they were appropriate for their mission. Vera also acted as liaison with the families of SOE agents, ensuring they received the proper pay.

Vera did not operate as a wireless operator or courier during her time with the SOE, but she still proved vital to the operation of the organization. She never deployed for a mission into enemy territory; she would often escort agents to the airfield from which they'd depart for France. Before they would leave for their mission, she carried out any final security checks before allowing them to depart. Her role was to make sure that the SOE agents were safe and taken care of wherever possible.

Vera typically showed up to the "F" Section's Baker Street office around 10:00 am every morning. She always attended the daily section heads meeting chaired by Buckmaster, often staying until late into the night to await the decoded transmissions sent by field agents. Her days were long, but full of purpose. She was not well liked among her colleagues, but Buckmaster trusted her integrity completely. He greatly respected her exceptional memory and organizational skills.

Throughout the war, she was Buckmaster's right-hand woman and the person responsible for organizing spy deployment. Her skills were needed within the organization and served the SOE well. Her time working for the "F" Section has since been looked on with a bit of controversy.

Although Vera was an integral part of the organization, she has been viewed with some scrutiny within certain circles in more recent years. There are questions as to how clues that one of "F" Section's main spy networks had been infiltrated by Germans had gone unnoticed by Buckmaster and Vera. It is posited that the two failed to pull agents out of danger, instead sending more agents into dangerous situations.

Vera received signals from captured radios that were not checked and failed to inform Buckmaster. It's alleged that, due to her negligence, she failed to keep Buckmaster from repeating past mistakes, putting agents at further risk.

It has been suggested that Vera, who still had relatives in Nazi-occupied Europe, may have been somewhat defensive about her past involvement with the Abwehr during the 1940 rescue of her cousin. She kept this involvement a secret from her colleagues at the SOE and it was only after the war that this came to light. Furthermore, Vera was a Romanian who had not obtained British citizenship for much of the war, making her legally an enemy alien and highly vulnerable.

Life After the War

Whatever the case regarding her wartime actions, it should be noted that Buckmaster was her superior officer and ultimately responsible for the decisions made regarding his agents. It is also worth noting that following the liberation of France and the Allied victory in Europe, Vera went to France and Germany, attempting to uncover the fates of the 51 "F" Section agents still unaccounted for after entering enemy territory. Even after the war was ending, she still seemed loyal to the agents she had taken care of.

Originally, she received little support in her task, and in fact, received some opposition to her work. As the atrocities of the Nazis became more well-known, there grew a popular demand for war crime trials. Due to this change of attitude, it was decided that official support would be given to Vera's mission.

In January of 1946, Vera arrived in Germany as a newly promoted Squadron Leader in the WAAF, now funded by MI6. She began her search for the missing agents, including 14 women. She searched for these missing operatives, but it was not the only role she played in post-war activities. She also carried out interrogations of Nazi war crime suspects and testified as a prosecution witness in the ensuing trials.

Vera returned to Britain in October of that same year, but the next month her commission was extended so she could return to Germany to assist the prosecution in the Ravensbrück trial, lasting until January 1947. She used this as an opportunity to continue her search for the missing spy Noor Inaya Khan (a subject in the previous volume), who she now knew had died at Dachau, not Natzweiler–Struthof, as was originally thought.

While tracing 117 of the 118 missing "F" Section agents, she was also able to determine the circumstances surrounding the deaths of all 14 women, 12 of whom had died in concentration camps. Following these discoveries, Vera was able to persuade the War Office to record these women as "killed in action," despite technically being civilians at the time of their deaths.

Not content to just uncover these women's fates, Vera made sure that their sacrifices were not forgotten or overlooked. She fought to make sure that they received official recognition from the British government for their bravery. She was the driving force behind many of these women being posthumously awarded with official honors and plaques to commemorate them. By 1947, Vera was demobilized and although she was nominated for the MBE, she was not awarded any honors in the postwar honors list. She was, however, awarded the Croix de Guerre in 1948.

Finally moving on from her intelligence work, Vera went to work for the United Nations Educational, Scientific, and Cultural Organization (UNESCO) Central Bureau for Educational Visits and Exchanges. She had the role of officer manager there from 1948, eventually becoming director in 1952. Following over a decade of service, Vera retired early in 1961, settling in East Sussex.

Along the way, she served as advisor on several films that followed the lives of female SOE spies. She advised on the movie *Odette* in 1950, and in 1958 she did the same for the movie *Carve Her Name with Pride*, about SOE agent Violette Szabo (also a subject of the previous volume). It would seem she was still unwilling to let the legacy of these brave women spies die out.

Vera passed away on June 24, 2000, at the age of 92. In the years preceding her death, she had received several honors that had been denied her immediately following the war. In 1987, she was made a Knight of the Legion of Honor by the French government, and 10 years later, she was appointed Commander of the Order of the British Empire in the 1997 Birthday Honors.

Although there is a lot of controversy swirling around this particular agent, it is undeniable the effect she had on the war efforts and beyond. She was a woman who took charge and dedicated herself to the cause. Whether or not she was negligent at times, her courage after the war, in searching for the missing agents despite backlash, cannot be denied. Were it not for her, many of those agents would be lost to time, with no awareness of their lives and fate. Vera undoubtedly left her mark and will not easily be forgotten for her contributions.

Chapter 7:

Elaine Marie Madden (May 7, 1923 to 2012)

Early Life

Elaine was born in Poperinghe, Belgium to Australian father, Larry Madden, and Belgian mother Caroline Duponselle. She was the couple's only child, and therefore grew up without any siblings for company. The couple attempted to have a second child, but Caroline died while miscarrying, when Elaine was only 9 years old. It was just her and her father facing the world together.

Larry Madden was employed by the Imperial War Graves Commission, a respectable career. He had a struggle that happened behind closed doors. He had always had a drinking problem, but it worsened after the loss of Caroline. His career with the Commission ended in March of 1932, though records are unclear on whether he left voluntarily or was dismissed.

Elaine's relationship with her father was far from ideal. While drunk, he would exclaim that he didn't want her because she looked too much like her mother. She was a constant reminder of the loss that he had suffered, and it ultimately damaged any relationship they could have had. Larry continued to spiral after his career ended, as he leaned into his drinking and gambling. Caroline's family stepped in, paying for him to go to Britain where he joined the army. Elaine lost touch with him following his enlistment.

Following her father's heartbreaking rejection, Elaine was sent to live with her grandparents, who were living in Poperinghe and owned the Palace Hotel in town. Initially schooled at the British Memorial School in Ypres, Elaine was eventually sent to a convent boarding school by her grandparents.

During her time at the convent school, Elaine was made to wear a uniform of thick black stockings and an ankle-length dress. A rebellious Elaine was not happy with this arrangement and after only a few weeks, cut her dress to knee length and her stockings to ankle length. The school did not look kindly on this act and contacted her grandparents, requesting that they remove her from the school. After just a short stint at the convent school, Elaine returned to the school in Ypres. There, she excelled and was made a prefect by her senior year.

Elaine eventually realized that her grandparents were caring for her not out of love, but out of a sense of obligation. Crushed by this realization, she was pleased to have the opportunity to leave for London, where she attended secretarial college. , she would not finish her education there. During a Christmas visit, she quarreled with her family regarding her education. Upset by the argument, Elaine decided she would not return to college, relieving the family of the burden of paying for it.

When she was 17, Elaine was engaged to Belgian officer Edgar Callant. , her life was disrupted shortly after when WWII spread to her country with the Nazi invasion of France, Belgium, and The Netherlands. With her aunt, only 19 herself, Elaine set off for the coast where the pair took part in the Dunkirk evacuation. They sheltered in a barn, where they were eventually discovered by three British soldiers. The five of them made their way to Dunkirk together.

Upon their arrival in Dunkirk, the five were greeted with a scene of chaos. As Elaine later recalled: "The whole place was on fire. I've never seen anything like it, even in films. I thought that my last moment had come" (Elliott & Fox, 2011). The soldiers gave the women their coats and tin helmets to disguise them as soldiers, standing around them to help them blend in. The women were spotted when climbing down a rope ladder into a trawler, given away when their legs were seen. Still, after Elaine told the captain she was British, he allowed them to use his cabin.

Elaine reached the United Kingdom safely and started staying with her aunt in Streatham upon her arrival. She got a position as a clerk for the British Relay Wireless Company. She spent her nights with the Women's Voluntary Services Air Raid Precautions personnel, searching for survivors in bombed out buildings during the Blitz.

Her work with Air Raid Precautions inspired Elaine to study for her Red Cross certificates in Home Nursing and First Aid. She wanted to be able to assist more practically with the wounded civilians. Later, Elaine recounted that she wasn't sure why, but she did not have much fear of the Blitz. This may have been why she was able to remain composed enough to take on the role she did.

Career as a Spy

At the start of 1944, 20-year-old Elaine was living in Bayswater with a roommate and began working with the Auxiliary Territorial Service around that time. She had a burning desire to be of greater service, something she mentioned to an American officer. He arranged a meeting for her, and she was subsequently recruited by the SOE. Elaine began working within the Belgian section of the organization. After being properly vetted, she was appointed to FANY, which was a common cover for female spies at the time.

In April of 1944, Elaine went to the Students' Assessment Board in Surrey. It was there she was given her cover name, "Elaine Meeus," with other false names for her falsified papers. She left her time there with fairly positive reviews from her superiors, who referred to her as "alert, efficient, and methodical" (Elliott & Fox, 2011). They also marveled at her ability to take quick, decisive action.

She still had more training ahead of her but in August of 1944, Elaine parachuted back into Belgium, one of just two women parachutists sent to the country. Her task, when she arrived, was to gather intelligence of V1 and V2 rocket launch sites. She also had a secondary mission, as she was tasked with protecting and arranging the escape of Prince Charles of Belgium, though she did not know his true identity. She knew him as "Monsieur Bernard."

Elaine began acting as courier for the experienced officer André Wendelen. Also, part of their team was wireless operator Jacques Van de Spiegel. Together, they conducted intelligence work in occupied Belgium. During this time, Elaine had several close calls, including a memorable incident when she was given a lift by a German officer when she had a radio receiver on her person. She was also followed on more than one occasion and had to improve in ditching her tails.

Not all of her time was filled with nail-biting missions. On September 3, 1944, she was present for the liberation of Brussels and joined in the ensuing festivities. Elaine was able to see the effects of the work being done. , it wasn't completely without the stress of war, as she and Wendelen were left to guard a British tank while an officer relieved some of his men. Right then, some Germans ran by and Wendelen shot his revolver while Elaine fired a gun on the tank.

Neither were successful in hitting their target, though Elaine sheepishly admitted later that she believed she had damaged a monument. In the aftermath, she discovered 'Bernard's' true identity. She was stunned and concerned that she'd been open about her criticism of his policies. When she asked what she should now call him, he replied: "Just call me Bernard, as usual" (Elliott, 2015). Elaine had earned the respect of a prince.

Elaine continued her spy work after the liberation of The Netherlands and eventually joined an SOE group led by René Verstrepen. The atmosphere was different here, the people more defeated. During her time with the group, she worked with wireless operator Michel Blaze as a coder. They operated out of the western Netherlands, providing information to the Canadian First Army.

During their service together, Elaine and Wendelen had become lovers. Their relationship would not last as events in Wendelen's life precluded a possibility of a future for the couple. Following Belgium's liberation, the government offered him the role of Belgian Ambassador to Austria. He took the role, and it ultimately spelled the end of the romance. An ambassador needed money and Wendelen had very little. Elaine had even less, making her a poor match for his new role. He proposed to a woman with means and warned Elaine of the news before it hit the papers.

Heartbroken, Elaine began a flirtatious relationship with Michel Blaze as she tried to stop holding a torch for her former lover. Their feelings for each other grew, as Blaze pursued her relentlessly. The two were engaged by December of 1944.

In early 1945, the network for which Elaine worked was lambasted in an internal memo. As a result, Elaine, Blaze, and two other members were dismissed and replaced with new agents. Elaine was taken aback at the news, unsure what she could have done to merit dismissal. She suspected it may have been due to her impending marriage, which was technically prohibited under Routine Order 32, which barred the union of active agents, deeming it a security risk. She had to reconcile with the only option she felt was available to her: resigning from the SOE. Elaine and Blaze, once free of the bureaucracy, married in March of 1945.

Leaving the SOE, Elaine still wanted to take part in the action, the type of work she had grown accustomed to while working for the agency. She was transferred to the Special Allied Airborne Reconnaissance Force (SAARF). As part of her role there, she was sent to Nazi concentration camps to find surviving SOE agents, resistance workers, and Belgian political prisoners. Her mission took her all over but did not prove overwhelmingly successful. She only freed two prisoners during her time with SAARF. As the war ended, the organization was disbanded, however, and Elaine had new horrors to face.

Life After the War

Elaine found herself haunted by the horrors she had seen in the concentration camps. She returned to the photographs she'd taken of the different camps regularly and had frequent nightmares about what she had witnessed. Her husband understood but in those early days back in Britain, she barely saw him. He was in Brussels negotiating his release from the Belgian army and scouting for peacetime jobs.

While Blaze was away, Elaine found herself suddenly jobless and homeless in London. An old friend offered her a place to stay, but she refused this. With everything that had happened, she needed a change of scenery. She needed something different. She wrote to her aunt in the northwest and asked to stay with her until Blaze either came back or called for her. Her aunt agreed and an exhausted Elaine showed up, glad for a respite.

While she was staying there, Elaine discovered that her aunt had burned the photographs of the concentration camps. Elaine protested, because the photographs were evidence. Her aunt was adamant, describing the toll she'd seen them take on Elaine. She wanted Elaine to accept the war was over and get back to normal. Normal was not something Elaine was sure she was capable of.

A short time later, she discovered she was pregnant. When she called Blaze in Brussels, he was delighted at the news. They had much to celebrate as he had found opportunities for peacetime work with Unilever. With this news and the impending arrival of the baby, Elaine decided to retire and focus on her family.

A while after the war ended, Elaine received the Croix de Guerre and was Mentioned in Dispatches for her service. She accepted the honors from her old friend 'Bernard,' whom she had not seen since learning of his true identity. Shortly after, she gave birth to her son, Lawrence Bernard Blaze. From then on, she lived a quiet life, enamored with her new role as a mother.

Elaine was undoubtedly a merit to the organizations with which she served. She was determined to help the fight against the fascist regime, even when obstacles stood in her path. She served the Allies well and was able to retire with a beautiful family, knowing her value to the war effort. She passed away in 2012, leaving behind quite a legacy.

Chapter 8:

Blanche Charlet (May 23, 1898 to October 11, 1985)

Early Life

Blanche Charlet was born Valentine Blanche Charlet on May 23, 1898, in London to Belgian parents. From the beginning she was dark haired, beautiful, and slight. Not much is known about her childhood. With this part of her life lost to time, it is hard to describe the events that shaped her as a young person. Without an idea of what kind of child she was, it's hard to understand her early pre-war years.

Before the outbreak of WWII, Blanche was living in Brussels, where she managed an art gallery. An intelligent woman, she had picked up several languages while working there, something that would suit her later work well. Her English was described as "passable" (Escott, 2012).

When WWII broke out, Blanche fled to London, where she had several contacts, despite being little more than a refugee. She was attracted to Ebury Court Hotel, with its mixed range of customers, eventually leading to her recruitment by the SOE.

Career as a Spy

When the SOE began recruiting women as operatives, Blanche was among the first to enter their ranks and one of the first four to be trained. Much like other women who worked for the SOE during the war, she enlisted in her cover organization FANY. By this time, Blanche was 43 years old but carried her years well. She was recognized for her lively manner and quick understanding by her trainers.

Her training went well, and the SOE saw her as a promising operative. It was agreed that she would be sent to France, though due to her age, she would be taken by sea rather than parachuting in. In August of 1942, she flew to Gibraltar where she boarded the *Seadog*, a felucca converted to military use that took her down the French Riviera. She finally arrived in Vichy, France on September 1st. Vichy was not yet occupied by the Nazis, though the threat was looming.

Her arrival went smoothly and Blanche, going by her cover name "Madame Sabine Lecomte," was able to spend the night in a quiet villa on the coast for the night before reporting. She was alone for the time being but was in possession of the name and address of another agent in Cannes.

The next day, she went to find the agent only to find that he had been arrested just the day before. She had narrowly missed sharing the same fate. Unsure of her next move, she cast around for other contacts in the days that followed but found none. Finally, feeling vulnerable, she decided to make her way to Lyon to another contact, Virginia Hall (see Chapter 16), who was expecting Blanche to be her replacement.

This turned out not to be the case and Blanche discovered she was to join the SOE's Ventriloquist network. The network was led by Philippe de Vomécourt (codename "Gauthier") and his second in command Aron (codename "Joseph"). Her first assignment in the network was to secure safe houses for their soon-to-arrive wireless operator, Brian Stonehouse.

This first task turned out to be not as easy as expected. Though it was not an occupied area, the Germans were watching Lyon carefully, believing it to be a hotbed of resistance activity. On top of this complication, Stonehouse was unlucky in his arrival. When he parachuted in, it took him several days to retrieve his wireless set, which had ended up suspended in a tree. Following this, he experienced technical difficulties and health problems, delaying his work within the network. After getting the new agent settled, Blanche was freed up for a role as the Ventriloquist network's courier.

Under the codename "Christianne," she began the important work of carrying intelligence between the agents. Before long, Blanche and Stonehouse grew to be discontented with the network. This was primarily due to the attitude of Vomécourt and his second in command, leading to disorganization in the group.

On October 24, 1942, Blanche was carrying a message from the network leader to be sent to London. Stonehouse was transmitting from a house at Feyzin, a location he was using for just the second time. As Blanche approached the house, she became uneasy at the sight of two trailers at the side of the road. Choosing caution, she took the papers she had been carrying and hid them in a shed behind the house.

She entered the house without the papers and found everything to be normal. Relieved that nothing seemed to be out of place, Blanche went outside to retrieve the papers she had stowed away and took them up to the attic of the house where Stonehouse was working. He was in the middle of transmitting, so she placed the messages beside him and went to work on her own coding.

A mere few minutes later, the lights abruptly went off in the house. The two immediately realized the danger and collected incriminating evidence of their activities. They hid the equipment and papers in the basement and decided to try to make an escape through the back door that led into the garden. The door was already guarded by the Gestapo and the two were arrested as they exited.

The house was searched after the arrest and evidence of their activities was discovered. Subsequently, Blanche was taken to the Petit Depot St

Jean in Lyon. On the trip there, she hid her notebook of addresses under the seat of the car. When she arrived at the depot, she and Stonehouse had only a few moments to get their stories straight before the inevitable interrogation. Blanche decided that she would tell the interrogators that she had no idea what a wireless operator was. She was just a mistress to a married man, whom she could not reveal lest she hurt his wife.

The French police, sympathetic to Blanche, were initially easy on her. Once they discovered her codename, they became harsher, and the interrogation went downhill with the Germans now present. Blanche stuck to the story of her innocence, pretending to faint, and playing the role of a simple woman, unaware of Resistance activities. She was interrogated for days, during which time she was imprisoned. During courthouse exercise, she was able to remain in contact with Stonehouse and they informed each other of what they had each said.

Eventually, the Germans had gathered enough evidence, and the two agents were transferred to the prison at Castres. The purpose of the prison was to hold prisoners who would be shot in retribution for any attacks on the Germans. Conditions were poor and morale low. Blanche's circumstances looked grim. During her time there, Blanche shared a cell with three other women with whom she got along. She had to remain vigilant for any possible informants within the prison.

Despite the conditions being poor and food being scarce, discipline was fairly lax in the prison. Blanche made a point of befriending other prisoners and even some staff members. One such staff member was Yugoslav, a cleaner. The evening of September 16, 1943, he informed her that they could have free run of the prison for several hours. Prisoners had been supplied with duplicate keys and pistols. Many of the guards had been locked up or tricked. Escape was possible. On that night, 37 prisoners were able to escape the prison, Blanche among them.

Blanche escaped with a fellow prisoner named Suzanne, and together the two were guided by a young man who promised to get them to the other escapees. The boy eventually admitted that he was hopelessly lost and struck off on his own. The women were left to their own devices.

Exhausted and hungry, they stopped in a nearby town and asked a priest for his help. He supplied them with food and allowed them to sleep in his barn. Not long after, though, Blanche began to worry that they had been betrayed so the two women fled once again. Two days later, the women were becoming desperate and decided to take a great risk. They rang the doorbell of a Benedectine monastery to ask for aid.

The occupants of the monastery were more than happy to help the two women and sent them to a pleasant guest house on the grounds. Within the monastery, they were met with utter kindness, despite the danger the monks were taking on by sheltering them. Blanche and her companion stayed there for 2 months, even eventually contacting the SOE.

At the beginning of January 1944, the women were instructed by a French escape line to make their way to Paris. Once they arrived safely, Blanche was sent to Lyon. She was not happy with this development, as she was known there. She would need to stay there for 2 months before moving to Jura. While in Jura, she had a little more freedom from danger and did a bit of work as a courier and escort.

In April of that year, the SOE arranged for Blanche and her companion to finally return to London through another escape line. The escape line took them across France to Brittany, where they were picked up and departed by boat. This was an incredibly dangerous operation, as the Germans were fortifying the coast in anticipation of an Allied invasion. Still, they made it through safely, arriving in England on April 20, 1944. After enjoying a decent breakfast, Blanche went to London to deliver her report.

Life After the War

After the war, Blanche received a special honor for her courageous service. She was made a Member of the Order of the British Empire, recognizing her bravery and chivalry during WWII. She did not receive any other honors, despite her courageous and fascinating stint as an SOE operative.

Not much is known about Blanche's life after the war. She lived a quiet life and never married or had children. Passing on in 1985 at the age of 87, she surely left a mark on the world with her brave service. It should be noted that Blanche was one of the oldest women spies sent into occupied territory. She kept up with her younger peers and accomplished much in her career.

Chapter 9:

Margery Myers Booth Strohm (1906 to April 11, 1952)

Early Life

Margery was born sometime in 1906 in Lancashire, the daughter of Levi and Ada Booth. The family later moved to Southport. Her education was thorough and varied. She first trained in Bolton with R. Evans, followed by Knightsbridge with Eilene O'Dorme. Finally, she landed at the Guildhall School of Music where she won a scholarship in 1925 and was discovered to be extremely talented as a singer. From there, she won the Opera Scholarship and the Liza Lehmann Prize. Her musical talent was unparalleled, and she had a promising career in the arts ahead of her.

Her career developed beautifully, with performances at Bayreuth and at the Berlin State Opera. By 1933, she was thriving as a celebrated opera singer. It was that year, after one of her performances, she would first begin thinking about the new Führer, Adolf Hitler, who was seated in the Royal Box for the evening.

While unwinding after the show, a knock came at the door. Margery was in her underwear but, assuming it was the bellboy Otto, she called out for the caller to enter. She was shocked when the door opened and there stood Hitler himself, flanked by two SS officers. They had with them a large bouquet of red roses wrapped in a German flag, the swastika symbol prominently displayed on it.

Fighting against a panic attack, Margery managed to handle the situation with grace. When the SS officers dismissed her maid, she demurely slipped into her dressing gown and invited the Führer inside. He praised her for her magnificent performance and after exchanging pleasantries, Hitler departed the dressing room with his SS officers in tow. Now alone in the dressing room, Margery put away the flag with the prominent swastika. The symbol had become known for the violence of the SS Officers, and she was uncomfortable with its presence.

When she read the card attached to the gift, however, she was in for another surprise. It was signed "With Love, from Hitler" and included a phone number (Harvey, 2015). What she didn't realize, as she slipped the card into her purse, was what a boon this would be for British intelligence one day. She was also blissfully unaware of what this bizarre encounter meant for her. The invite to brush shoulders with the enemy made her an enticing candidate for MI6 recruitment.

Forgetting about the strange event, which undoubtedly made for good dinner party conversation, Margery continued with her opera performances, taking several notable roles, before eventually moving back to London to continue her career in Covent Garden in 1936. , she would find herself in Germany after marrying Egon Strohm, the heir to a vast beer fortune.

Her talent was renowned and her career thrived in Germany, with performances at Bayreuth and with the Berlin State Opera. She had a gilded life but something would soon happen that would change its direction. With the tensions leading up to WWII building, the world was scrambling to respond. Margery found herself in the middle of the intelligence network quite unexpectedly.

Career as a Spy

It happened when Margery was back in London for the funeral of a friend. She was in a little licensed cafe in the West End enjoying a coffee when a stranger approached her and addressed her by name. He had come to her with an invitation. He was a mediary for his captain in an organization that aided the Jewish people escape the persecutions of Germany.

She agreed to meet with the captain who informed her that war was inevitable and right on the horizon. They wanted her to aid them in their intelligence work in response to the impending threat. Margery was shocked that they would choose her but to them it was practical. She moved in high Nazi circles and had many influential connections through her wealthy husband. She had access to intelligence with ease and they wanted her to use those circumstances to their advantage.

Their logic and call to human decency softened Margery toward their cause and she began giving small insights into the circles with which she was engaged. They were delighted, as it was exactly the type of intelligence they were hoping to gain from her participation. Margery was the closest person to Hitler to whom they had access, making her invaluable to their intelligence work.

She decided to take them up on their offer and was given the codename "Zeus" before leaving that day. She was also given a name for an important contact. Margery had just joined MI6, the British government's special branch for intelligence.

Because she was so well liked among Nazi circles, Margery was given a lot of trust among those closest to Hitler. This meant she could easily keep an eye out for trouble in the very belly of the beast. She knew how to get the intelligence she sought and whom to listen to at the right moments. She was the perfect plant.

Her task was tricky. She had to cozy up to these men and learn their secrets. She had to learn their secrets and plans by making them think she was one of them. Loved for her singing, she often sang for the SS officers and even Hitler himself on more than one occasion. After the outbreak of WWII, Margery was invited into his inner circle at the Wolf's Lair and at Berchesgarten.

By this point in Margery's career, MI6 had trained her in the operation of wireless operators and how to conceal them. With this training, the organization had essentially placed a master spy among Hitler's ranks. She would take in the conversations of the powerful men around her and transmit the intelligence back to the London office, allowing them to properly strategize. The work could get dangerous, of course. In one particular incident, she sang for Hitler with secret documents hidden in her undergarments, earning her the affectionate nickname 'Knickers Spy' after the war.

, her good luck and skill at charming the inner circle would soon come to an end. In early 1944, Margery fell under suspicion and was captured by the Gestapo. They tortured her for information but when it failed to prove anything, they let her go. Upon her release, she made her way west. She was liberated in Germany by the advancing United States army. The war ended with her safe from the dangerous crowd she had infiltrated for years.

Life After the War

Margery was affectionately known in the intelligence community after the war as the 'Knickers Spy.' Her contributions had made a great difference in the war against the threatening Nazi regime and those who knew were enamored with her particular brand of spying. She lived a quiet life after the war, emigrating to New York.

Unfortunately, Margery did not have long to enjoy the post-war world. She was reportedly diagnosed with terminal breast cancer in the years following and died from it on April 11, 1952, at the age of 46. Though she did not live long, she left an indelible mark on the world. Her bravery in the Wolf's Lair made it possible for British forces to properly strategize around their enemy. She could easily have ridden out the war in relative comfort, one of Hitler's favorites. Instead, she saw the wrong being committed and put herself in harm's way for the greater good.

Undoubtedly, her bravery deserves to be remembered. She won no medals or honors for her time serving MI6, which seems to many a major oversight. There might be bureaucratic reasons for this but she remains undecorated to this day.

In more recent years, her contributions have received more recognition. In 2010, special photographs of the well-revered spy were auctioned off, bringing attention to her accomplishments. In 2014, a movie was made of her extraordinary life, entitled *Margery Booth: A Spy in the Eagle's Nest*. A book by the same name followed. Finally, people were beginning to learn the story of Hitler's favorite opera singer, who brought him down from the inside.

Her legacy lives on in the post-war world not just through books and movies. Her contributions were undoubtedly some of the most valuable, coming directly from the source. Her courage to smile in the face of the world's greatest enemy while secretly informing him is not just commendable, it's almost unfathomable. She chose a life of purpose over a life of comfort.

Chapter 10:

Nancy Grace Augysta Wake

(August 13, 1912 to August 7, 2011)

Early Life

Nancy Wake was born in Wellington, New Zealand on August 13, 1912, the youngest of six children for her parents Charles and Ella Wake. She was Māori and barely grew up in the area before the family moved to Australia and settled in North Sydney when she was only 2 years old. Shortly after their arrival, Charles left the family to return to New Zealand. Ella was now caring for the children on her own.

It was in Australia that Nancy grew up, looked after by her unflappable mother. While in Sydney, she attended North Sydney Household Arts (Home Science) School. This type of education proved not to serve Nancy's vision of her life. She ran away from home at 16 to work as a nurse.

With money she had inherited from her aunt, Nancy traveled to New York and then to London. Though initially working as a nurse, she changed course again and tried her hand at journalism. She was a woman looking for a purpose. She had no way of knowing that when the next great war arrived, she would find one.

In the 1930s, Nancy worked in Paris and then for Hearst in New York as a European correspondent. Her travels gave her a worldly attitude that served her well in her later career in intelligence work. She witnessed Hitler's rise to power and saw the horrors that were building in the world around her. She knew a storm was coming.

Before the war had even begun, Nancy sprang into action. She met a wealthy French industrialist—Henri Edmond Fiocca—whom she eventually married in 1939. They were living together in Marseilles, France when Germany invaded. After the fall of France in 1940, Nancy joined the escape network headed by Captain Ian Garrow, which became known as the Pat O'Leary Line. She worked as a courier for the network, delivering equipment, messages, and subversive literature. She also escorted those escaping through the line.

Nancy was phenomenal at avoiding capture during her time with the network. The Gestapo called her the "White Mouse" for her ability to elude danger. The resistance had to be careful with her missions. She had grown a reputation and the Gestapo were on the lookout for the little mouse.

In 1942, the network was betrayed and the Pat O'Leary Line collapsed. Nancy, wise to what this meant for the members of the organization, fled France in the aftermath. Her husband chose to stay behind, a decision that would ultimately cost him his life later on in the war. Nancy made her way to Britain and to a new destiny.

Career as a Spy

Upon arrival in Britain, Nancy joined the SOE, where she was trained in several different programs. Vera Atkins was particularly impressed with her, remarking that everything she did, she did well. Her training reports were equally glowing, calling her a good shot and observing she excelled in fieldcraft. She was even noted as having put the men to shame during training. Nancy had finally found her calling.

In late April of 1944 Nancy, along with three others, parachuted into south-central France as part of the Freelance team, headed by John Hind Farmer (codename "Hubert"). Nancy's landing was far from flawless, as Resistance leader Henri Tardivat found her tangled in a tree shortly after her landing. Upon his discovery, he remarked: "I hope that all the trees in France bear such beautiful fruit this year." To this, Nancy replied: "Don't give me that French shit" (*Nancy Wake*, 2011).

The team had been sent into the area to serve as a liaison between London and the local Maquis group led by Émile Coulaudon (codename "Gaspard"). Their initial relationship with the Maquis leader was frosty at best. He wanted the arms and the money from the Allies but was uncooperative until the French Forces of the Interior in London stepped in and instructed him to work with the agents.

With the Gaspard situation squared away, the SOE began sending in large amounts of arms, money, and equipment. During this time, it was Nancy's responsibility to pinpoint where the shipments would land, collect them, and allocate them among the Maquis. She was also responsible for distributing pay to individual soldiers. While she carried out this work, she kept with her a list of the targets the Maquis were to destroy before the Allied invasion of France. These targets were essential to German communication and destroying them would hinder their chances of a response to the invasion.

, on May 20, 1944, disaster began brewing. Gaspard arrogantly declared a general mobilization of Resistance fighters, assembling over 7,000 men over the three groups. It was his objective to demonstrate that the Resistance was capable of liberating areas from the Germans without outside help. On June 2, the Germans launched a probing attack on his base at Mont Mouchet. On the 10th, they launched a larger scale attack and, on the 20th, they managed to encircle Gaspard's positions, forcing his forces to flee after suffering heavy casualties.

During this devastating attack, the others knew that they needed to be in contact with the SOE in London. The closest radio and operator were in Châteauroux, a far distance to travel. Not to be deterred, Nancy borrowed a bicycle and rode it to Châteauroux and found a radio. She reached out to London and then traveled back by bicycle once more, traveling around 310 miles in less than 72 hours.

After the determined bicycle ride that surely aided the Allies in strategically responding, Nancy rejoined her group and they joined up with Henri Tardivat's Resistance group, which had just acquired a new operator. The operator was named Roger, a 19-year-old American marine. The next month, two more Americans joined their team as instructors, Reeve Schley, and John deKoven Alsop. Neither spoke much French but they both proved themselves as effective trainers.

While working with Tavidat's group, Nancy reportedly helped inflate a series of attacks on German convoys and fought off an attack on their camp by the Germans, in which seven French Maquis were killed. Her primary role, though, continued to be the reception and distribution of air-dropped supplies that arrived nearly every night.

According to Nancy, she once discovered that the men were using three of the women as sex workers and mistreating them. She managed to coerce the Maquis to release the women, whom she gave a wash and fresh clothes. She let two of the girls free but suspected that the third was a German spy. She interrogated her and the truth was revealed. Nancy told the Maquis that they needed to execute her, given the information she had most likely gathered. The men hesitated until Nancy said she would perform the execution herself. They finally capitulated and before the execution, the woman spat in Nancy's face and stripped naked to face the firing squad. Looking back, Nancy had no regrets about the execution.

France was invaded by American troops as part of Operation Dragoon on August 15, 1944, and the Resistance groups harassed the retreating Germans. Her friend in the Resistance group, Tardivat, was wounded in these attempts and eventually lost a leg to amputation for his trouble. It was during the victory in Vichy that Nancy finally learned of the fate of her husband, a heartbreaking moment in the midst of such joy. In mid-September, Nancy and other members of the Freelance network returned to Great Britain, their job completed.

Life After the War

Immediately following the end of the war, Nancy was presented several honors and awards. Her service was highly regarded and she was given the George Medal, the Medal of Freedom, the Resistance Medal, and the Croix de Guerre, making her one of the most decorated female spies in WWII. Her bravery and quick thinking had been recognized and she was treated thus.

Following the war, Nancy continued to work in intelligence. Her skills were utilized by the intelligence department at the British Air Ministry, attached to embassies in Paris in Prague. With this position, Nancy was able to stay within her wheelhouse for a time after the Nazi regime was no longer a looming threat. She also tried her hand at politics, running as a Liberal party candidate in the Australian federal election for the Sydney seat of Barton in 1949 and again in 1951. She lost by a marginal number of votes both times, doing slightly better in 1951.

Following the 1951 election loss, Nancy moved back to England. She once again took up work as an intelligence officer, this time in the department of the Assistant Chief of the Air Staff at the Air Ministry in Whitehall. She remained in their service until marrying RAF officer John Forward, after which she resigned in 1957. The couple relocated to Australia in the early 1960s.

Upon returning to Australia, Nancy's interest in politics was rekindled. She was endorsed again as a Liberal candidate for the 1966 federal election for the Sydney seat of Kingsford Smith. Despite a close race, Nancy lost the election again. Around 1985, Nancy and her husband left Sydney to retire in Port Macquarie. It was during this year that she released her autobiography, *The White Mouse*, named for the old nickname given to her by the Gestapo.

Nancy's husband passed away in 1997 after 40 years of marriage. Following his death, Nancy sold off her hard-earned war medals to support herself, saying: "There was no point in keeping them. I'll probably go to hell and they'd melt away" (Stafford, 2011). In 2011, she left Australia for the last time, bound for London. Upon arrival, she became a resident of the Stafford Hotel in St. James' Place. The hotel had formerly been a British and American forces club during the war, so it seems a suitable place for her to settle. She could be found in the lounge during the mornings, sipping a gin and tonic and regaling the other guests with her many war stories. She was well loved by the occupants and the hotel staff and when she held her 90th birthday there, the hotel picked up much of the cost.

Eventually, Nancy decided to move to the Royal Star and Garter Home for Disabled Ex-Service Men and Women in London. She spent the remainder of her life at the facility, undoubtedly continuing to tell her war stories to whomever would listen. Nancy passed away of a heart infection on August 11, 2011, at the age of 98. Following her death, several respected papers published obituaries outlining her wartime accomplishments.

Nancy was an effective agent. She was stealthy, quick-thinking, and a good shot. With her skillset, she was the perfect choice for spy work and she gave everything she had during her service. After a time of wandering in her youth, she found a career that was made for her. Even after the war, she remained in the intelligence game and following her retirement, told her war stories to whomever showed interest. She was proud of her work, and for good reason. Nancy was an incredible contributor to the fight against the Nazi regime.

Chapter 11:

Lise de Baissac (May 11, 1905 to March 29, 2004)

Early Life

Lise was born on May 11, 1905, in Mauritius, an island British colony off the coast of Africa. Her parents were Marie Louis Boucherville Baissac and Marie Louise Jeannette Dupont, who had two other children, both boys: Jean and Claude. The family were large landowners in Mauritius and considered British subjects, as everyone in the colony was. Lise grew up comfortably in her hometown but the family eventually moved to Paris when she was 14.

It was in Paris that she met her future husband when she was 17 years old. His name was Gustave Villameur, a penniless artist. Because of his financial and social standing, Lise's mother disapproved of their romance. To keep the two apart, she sent Lise to Italy, where she spent some time. When Lise returned to Paris, she took a position in an office, despite it being unusual for upper-class women to work at this time in history.

When Paris was occupied by the Germans in 1940, her eldest brother Jean enlisted in the British Army, ready to meet the ever-growing threat of the fascist regime. Lise, along with her younger brother, meanwhile traveled to southern France in hopes of reaching England and safety. The American Consulate aided her with her travel arrangements and the two siblings made their way to Spain, where they waited 5 months for permission to travel to the United Kingdom. In September of 1941, the pair arrived in Scotland, and from there Lise made her way to London.

Through her family connections, Lise was able to obtain a job at the *Daily Sketch*. Meanwhile, her younger brother was recruited by the SOE. Mauritians made great agents because of their proficiency in both English and French. Claude was an optimal recruit for the organization. At the time of his recruitment, the SOE was not yet actively recruiting women, so Lise remained with her job and waited for the moment when she could take part in the action.

Career as a Spy

As soon as the SOE began recruiting women, Lise took initiative and applied immediately. Her interview was conducted by Selwyn Jepson, who approved her for training in May of 1942. Her training took place at Beaulieu, Hampshire where she participated with the second group of women to be recruited by the SOE. Among her fellow trainees were Odette Sansom (Chapter 4), Mary Herbert (Chapter 13), and Jacqueline Nearne.

During her training, Lise was described as being difficult but dedicated to the cause. She was confident and intelligent, causing the SOE to see her great potential. In Lise's case, the SOE made a notable exception. Typically, within the organization, women were utilized as couriers or wireless operators. Lise was recognized as having the ability to head her own network, something that would come to pass before the war ended.

Lise received her first mission in September of 1942. On the night of the 25th, she and Andrée Borrel became the first women to parachute into occupied France. Borrel was the first to drop into the area with Lise right behind her, both landing in the village Bois Renard near the town of Mer. The two women were met by Resistance leader Pierre

Culioli. While Borrel departed for Paris to work for the Prosper network, Lise headed for Poitiers.

In Poitiers, Lise took up the role of courier and liaison officer for her brother Claude's Scientist network, a network specifically handling information regarding the Allied development of the first atomic bomb. It was her job to communicate messages to other Resistance networks. Eventually her mission gave way to forming a new circuit and to organize the pick-up of arms drops coming in from the United Kingdom. Her one-woman network was called Artist and Lise operated under the cover that she was a poor widow from Paris, "Madame Irene Brisse," seeking refuge and avoiding the food shortages in the capital. She took up residence at a small apartment on a street near Gestapo headquarters and would often exchange greetings with the Gestapo chief, Herr Grabowski.

Lise was something of an anomaly in the intelligence profession. She preferred to work alone whenever she could, and typically avoided the company of other SOE agents, except on rare occasions when she visited them on business in Paris or Bordeaux. She turned down an offer from the SOE to send her a wireless operator and rarely ever saw her brother. She was comfortable with missions on her own and saw no need for involvement with other agents.

Lise spent 11 months in Poitier, during which she received and briefed 13 newly arrived SOE agents. She also organized departures of Resistance leaders, agents, and others who were clandestinely traveling to England. During this time, she played the role of an amateur archaeologist, the perfect pretense for her frequent travels around the country on bicycle, identifying possible parachute drop-zones and landing areas.

Collecting supplies and arms dropped into the zones by Allied forces, Lise began transporting them to safehouses, where she distributed them. Along the way, she created a Resistance network of her own, recruiting a number of helpers who were sympathetic to the cause. One such helper was a teenage girl who accompanied Lise on much of her travels, assisting where she could. Lise, wary of SOE connections, was creating her own grassroots Resistance.

Since she had no wireless operator at her disposal, Lise communicated with London by traveling to Paris or Bordeaux, where her brother was organizing sabotage missions and gathering information. In June 1943, , her missions became more dangerous. Many members of the Prosper network were arrested and her Artist network was also penetrated by the Gestapo, which increased her risk of capture. In mid-August, Lise and her brother were flown back to England by Lysander, alongside SOE deputy head Nicholas Bodington. Upon her return, she became a conducting officer to two new agents, Yvonne Baseden and Violette Szabo.

While training the new agents, Lise had a parachuting accident and broke her leg. This delayed her return to France until she was fully healed. Finally, in April of 1944, she was able to return to her mission. , because of her injury, she was unable to parachute in. Instead, she was flown in by Lysander, landing in a farm field near Villers-les-Ormes in the middle of the night.

This time, Lise's mission was to act as courier for the Pimiento network, headed by Anthony Brooks and operating out of Toulouse. Her new codename for the mission was "Marguerite." Lise soon became frustrated at the trivial tasks she was being assigned within the network. Clever and ambitious, she felt her abilities were being wasted. The tension was somewhat mutual and she departed the network to help her brother Claude, who had recreated the Scientist network, now in southern Normandy.

As part of the new Scientist network, Lise acted as courier for her brother. To deliver messages, she would often bicycle 62 miles in a single day. She was also attempting to restrain now armed and over-zealous Resistance fighters from prematurely attacking the Germans and their infrastructure. The network's main job was to identify large open locations that could be used as possible landing spots for invading Allies or drop spots for supplies.

Lise, still living her cover as a poor widow, based herself in the village Saint-Aubin-du-Désert, where she had rented a second floor of a house. On June 5, 1944, she was in Paris attempting to recruit Resistance fighters. That evening, she heard the BBC broadcast the code word that indicated the Allied invasion was imminent. Upon hearing it, she immediately left by bicycle to get back to her network. It was a 190-mile trip that was not without risk. She passed through large formations of the German army on several occasions and slept in ditches as she went.

Finally arriving at her base near Normandy, Lise gathered information on German dispositions and passed it along to the Allies. Once again, Lise was at extreme risk of capture. She mentioned several incidents throughout the war when Germans tossed her room or tried to confiscate her bicycle, suspicious of her movements. On one memorable occasion, Lise accompanied a group of Maquis in engaging a German patrol in a firefight. The group was able to kill several Germans in the assault.

The 2 months after the Normandy landings were a hectic time for the Scientist network, as they gathered supply canisters at night and worked to impede the arrival of German reinforcements through sabotage. Lise also carried messages to the Allies just a few miles away now, providing them with intelligence on German movements.

On July 25, 1944, the United States army launched Operation Cobra, forcing the German army to rapidly retreat from the Scientist area of operation. The next month, Lise and her brother linked up with a lead unit of United States soldiers. Just a few days later, they were flown back to England, their mission having finally concluded.

, the two siblings made a quick return to France the following month for a single purpose: to find Mary Herbert (see Chapter 13). France was now liberated from German occupation so they were able to safely search for her. Claude had fathered a child with Herbert, Claudine, but he and the SOE lost contact with her. They were determined to find her, tracing her movements from Bordeaux to Poitiers. They finally located Herbert and her daughter in a house near Poitiers and she returned with them to England.

Life After the War

Lise was recognized for her work during the war with honors from the French and United Kingdom governments. France awarded her the Légion d'honneur and the Croix de Guerre, while the United Kingdom appointed her a Member of the Order of the British Empire. Truly, as a woman who had not only aided several networks but ran her own, she deserved the honors bestowed. Her work was extensive and fearless.

After the war ended, Lise hung up her spy skills and took a job with the British Broadcasting Corporation (BBC). At some point she reunited with her old flame Gustave Villameur, now a successful artist and interior designer living in Marseilles. In 1950 the two were married. Villameur died in 1978 and afterward, Lise lived alone in their magnificent apartment.

She gave a few interviews over the course of her life, recounting the work she did with the SOE. In one interview, she admitted that the "loneliness of a secret life" was one of her strongest emotions. She also dismissed the idea that bravery was the most necessary as she relied more on "cold-blooded efficiency" (O'Connor, 2014). After a long and fulfilling life, Lise passed away at the age of 98 on March 29, 2004.

Lise was in a league of her own when it came to the intelligence game. She knew the risks but she heard the call. Understanding that she had the necessary skills and disposition to take on this career, she jumped into the fray. Call it bravery or call it "cold-blooded efficiency" but Lise had the makings of a great spy and helped bring an end to a fascist regime.

Chapter 12:

Phyllis Latour (April 2, 1921 to present)

Early Life

Phyllis Latour was born in Durban, South Africa on April 2, 1921, the daughter of a French doctor and his wife Louise, who was a British citizen living in South Africa for the time being. Phyllis would never get a chance to know her father. Just 3 months after her birth, he died in French Equatorial Africa. Her mother remarried when Phyllis was 3 years old.

As Phyllis grew up in South Africa, her friends and family affectionately called her "Pippa." With her mother's new marriage, things seemed to be going well. The family was content. It would seem that her life had settled but there was more tragedy on the horizon for young Phyllis.

Phyllis's stepfather was a race car driver, something that enamored her mother. A bold woman, she would occasionally race his cars as well, something that was almost completely unheard of at the time. During one of these races, Louise's car malfunctioned and she was killed when it smashed into a barrier. After this terrible loss, young Phyllis went to live with her cousin for a time in the Congo.

In later interviews, Phyllis described her cousin and his wife as the only parents she really knew. She enjoyed her time with them immensely, feeling like part of the family. There would be another heartbreaking development in Phyllis's life. One day when she was 7, her cousin's wife went riding as she always did. The day took a troubling turn when the horse returned without her. It took a while for Phyllis's new 'mother' to be discovered but when they found her, she was dead, having been thrown from her horse.

Despite all of this tragedy so early on in her life, Phyllis claimed she had a happy childhood. She grew up with much affection from her 'big brothers.' They were all much older than her and she described it as having four fathers. They played with her and hugged her often, giving her a feeling of safety and warmth. They even taught the young Phyllis to shoot, something that would serve her well, later in her career. Eventually, Phyllis moved back to South Africa, where she stayed until moving to England in 1941.

Career as a Spy

Upon arriving in England, Phyllis immediately began aiding the war effort, joining the WAAF in November of 1941. She did well there, among the first to be trained to become a flight mechanic on airframes. Her skills served the WAAF well, but the SOE had taken notice of the young woman. Her skills, patriotism, and fluency in French made her a prime candidate for their recruitment.

Phyllis was recruited to the intelligence organization in 1943, and by November she had begun training as a wireless operator. Her training went well but her deployment was rushed. With D-Day looming, they needed more wireless operators on the ground and so they decided to send her into occupied territory earlier than her superiors would have liked.

Parachuting into Normandy on May 1, 1944, Phyllis landed in a dangerous area thick with German soldiers. For this reason, she had trouble dropping in because the reception party kept having to douse their lights. After three false action signals, she arrived. Even so, her landing didn't go off without a hitch. She ended up landing more than three fields away and had to find the reception party in the dark.

Her mission upon arrival was to aid Claude de Baissac's second Scientist network - the first one had been compromised by the Gestapo. Scientist II was based in Bordeaux but reached from Paris to the Pyrénées. She had been given a cover story by her superiors but unhappy with it, she falsified papers to fit her own story. She was to act as a student who left Paris to study art. She obtained papers from the Caen Mayor's office saying she was an art student in Caen, to add legitimacy to her story.

She first contacted London 2 days after her arrival from the house of a local doctor. She moved her operations to de Baissac's remote farmhouse after being warned the doctor's house was most likely being watched. A week later, de Baissac left for Paris and Phyllis went to Caen with Dandicolle, helping him make contacts for his stay there.

Late in May, it was discovered that there had been a German spy at her reception and they had discovered her parachute at the landing site. Concerned about these implications, Phyllis and Dandicolle hurriedly cleared out the farmhouse headquarters and sent a message to de Baissac and his sister (his courier and assistant) to avoid the house. Leaving the base behind, they set up shop in an old barn. Shortly after making the barn habitable for the agents, Phyllis took a bicycle ride to look for suitable sites for several wirelesses, so that in an emergency, she would have one readily available to her.

D-Day took place on Jun 6, 1944, with Allied forces dropping into Normandy. This was something that would ultimately turn the tide of the war and shortly afterward, de Baissac sent Dandicolle and another agent to establish the sub-network, Verger. Their role was to arm the local Maquis and encourage sabotage actions. The sub-network did well until July, when they were betrayed and shot, right before they were set to return.

Because of this tragic turn of events, Phyllis became even more indispensable to de Baissac, as she was his main contact with London. At the start, Phyllis was overwhelmed by the growing stakes and the new responsibilities but she soon found the confidence necessary to persevere. Furthermore, de Baissac provided her with guards to protect her, particularly when she was sending messages back to London.

Throughout her service, she had a number of close calls. Phyllis was a quick thinker who knew how to get out of tight spots. On one occasion, she was interrupted by two German soldiers looking for food. She began pretending to pack a suitcase (really her case for her wireless) and explained to the soldiers that she was arranging to go home as she had scarlet fever. Hearing the troubling diagnosis, the Germans quickly left and Phyllis escaped capture.

Following the D-Day landings, Phyllis and de Baissacs kept their distance from each other, in order to operate more safely. They only met when necessary, as every meeting carried significant risk. It was necessary to keep all involved safe.

As time marched forward, Phyllis began traveling more, especially when the Germans began moving closer. She was becoming confident in her abilities and figured she would be able to avoid any possible capture. This hubris concerned de Baissacs, who felt that she was bordering on recklessness with her safety.

de Baissacs ended up further north, which was overrun by the British Army by this point. They both felt safer in this new reality and even felt comfortable wearing their uniforms out in the open. Phyllis was a little behind them and was overrun by American soldiers in August. They held her prisoner for 5 hours, due to the fact she didn't match the description they had of her. A guide who knew Phyllis recognized her and she was released. She left to watch the armies depart on their mission to liberate the whole of France.

Life After the War

Following her service in the war, several honors and awards were bestowed on the courageous spy. Phyllis was awarded the 1939–1945 Star, the France and Germany Star, the Defense Medal, and the War Medal by the United Kingdom's government. She was also honored by the French government with the Légion d'honneur. Highly decorated, it was clear to those around her that she was a force to be reckoned with and a highly valuable operative during the war.

With WWII in her rearview mirror, Phyllis married an engineer by the name of Patrick Doyle. The two of them were somewhat nomadic, living in Kenya, Fiji, and Australia in the ensuing years. She now lives in Auckland, New Zealand where she has been settled for some time.

Phyllis has given a few interviews in the decades since the war, though she often doesn't want to discuss her wartime activities. In fact, her own family discovered the truth by reading it on the internet in 2000. Phyllis seems content to leave that part of her life firmly in the past. She is still alive, having celebrated her 100th birthday in April of 2021.

Phyllis is a bit of an anomaly. Her superiors were concerned about her lack of training when they sent her into the thick of the fight. She adapted well and recovered from setbacks with quick thinking. Their earliest assessment of her proved to be accurate. She was a skilled and intelligent agent that served the SOE well. Her brave decision to take up the call and her continued courage while she served makes her a fascinating woman, deserving of honor.

Chapter 13:

Mary Katherine Herbert (October 1, 1903 to January 23, 1983)

Early Life

Mary Katherine Herbert was born in Ireland, the daughter of Brigadier General Edmund Herbert and his wife. She was their youngest daughter. Due to her father's connections and wealth, she grew up comfortably, wanting for nothing.

Not much is known about her blessed childhood though it is likely she was well cared for and enjoyed powerful connections through her family. Little can be said about what kind of child she was. There are very few remaining documents about her early years. Therefore, I'm unable to tell you much about her early days. Her relationship with her family is a mystery lost to time and her childhood disposition is something we will likely never know.

Despite the lack of information on her early days, we do know that she was well educated. She was initially enrolled at the Slade School of Art, showing a particular talent for the arts. Later she would achieve a degree at London University, becoming fluent in several languages: French, Italian, Spanish, and German. She also received a diploma from the University of Cairo in Arabic. Her linguistic skills undoubtedly made her a prime candidate for SOE recruitment later down the line.

At the outbreak of WWII, Mary was in high demand. She was initially working in the British Embassy in Warsaw but later took a position as a civilian translator in the Air Ministry in London. Wanting to do her part for the effort, she later joined the WAAF on September 19, 1941, as a General Duties and Intelligence Clerk.

Career as a Spy

In March of 1942, Mary was released from the WAAF at her own request, following a pre-dated Section Officer commission from the SOE. She had the distinction of being the first WAAF officer to volunteer for the SOE. Like many other female agents in the intelligence organization, she was given extra cover through FANY, where she could be trained in arms and be sent abroad.

Mary joined three other women for her training course: Lise de Baissac (Chapter 11), Odette Sansom (Chapter 4), and Jacqueline Nearne. She was being trained to act as a courier for Resistance networks in occupied territory. During her time in the program, the SOE noted her inconspicuous looks and demeanor, which stood out to them as a good quality in an intelligence operative. She completed her training successfully in October with the confidence of the SOE that she would do well.

Shortly after her training was completed, Mary traveled by cramped submarine from England to Gibraltar. From there, she boarded a felucca headed to the southern coast of France, arriving on the night of October 31, 1942. The next morning, she boarded a train to Cannes, where she met with the others in the back of a salon. Still not at her destination, Mary took a train north toward Bordeaux, traveling into occupied territory. This was a dangerous undertaking but her forged papers kept her safe from detection as she traveled.

Mary finally reached Bordeaux in December of 1942, meeting the leader of the Scientist network, Claude de Baissac, for the first time. Upon her arrival, she discovered she wasn't the only new arrival. The other new members of the network were Roger Landes, a wireless operator, and Charles Hayes, a demolitions expert.

Mary was given the cover of "Madame Marie-Louise Vernier" (codename "Claudine") and all contact with de Baissac went through her. Although de Baissac was considered by SOE head Maurice Buckmaster to be one of his most difficult operatives, Mary got along quite well with him. This worked out well as they often worked closely together, with Mary having the responsibility of carrying messages, wireless sets, and equipment to Resistance members who required them. She also spent a decent amount of time searching for potential safehouses and landing sites for new recruits. She was often present as part of the reception party when new agents dropped into the area.

As the Scientist network expanded rapidly, Mary found herself traveling more than ever, covering a lot of ground to deliver her messages and arrange the designated drops. When she spent time in Poitiers, she met Lise de Baissac, Claude de Baissac's sister who rarely saw her brother due to security concerns. It became Mary's favorite stop and she would often carry messages between the two.

Claude de Baissac often took Mary with him when he visited Paris, as having a woman with him would help him avoid German security checks. As predicted, Mary's unassuming looks served well and he helped de Baissac avoid detection. She eventually found herself in a hotel in Paris that wasn't too concerned with registration. This proved useful when Landes required a new wireless set and the only replacement was in Paris, where he would check and carry back the new item.

By 1943, the Scientist network had built up a reputation for their sabotage schemes. Bolstered by their successes, London began generously supplying them with explosives and armaments. The ensuing sabotage carried out by the network was well timed and soured the Spanish–German negotiations over trains running between Bordeaux and Spain.

The sabotage was going well with at least one tactic - it was leaving the Germans harried and frustrated. It was also bringing unwanted attention to the network. Due to this danger, de Baissac was recalled to London in March of 1943 for briefing. This development signaled to the network and Resistance members that the Allied invasion was on the horizon, especially upon his return a month later.

, not long after, trouble found the hardworking network. In late June, the Gestapo stepped up their efforts in Paris and began rounding up members of the Physician network. It was inevitable that the Gestapo would use torture to reveal information that could lead them to the Scientist network, so the members were told to take cover, Mary among them. Unfortunately, the Gestapo had a run of good luck and discovered a list of members in a Bordeaux resident's home. Mary was shaken by the news and quickly moved to another apartment, changing her appearance, and adopting a new identity.

While Claude de Baissac made efforts to extract his network members from the danger zone, Mary traveled back and forth attempting to hold together the fraying edges of the extensive network. News soon reached them that arrests were being made in Lise de Baissac's network. The danger was creeping nearer and there was no ignoring it.

With the networks in chaos and confusion, Claude de Baissac was called back to London in mid-August. Many suspected that he would take Mary with him. They were, after all, close, and Mary desperately needed the break. , de Baissac decided to take his sister Lise with him, instead. This left André Grandclément as the new temporary leader of Scientist. This was a wildly unpopular move and to no one's surprise London quickly appointed Roger Landes as the new leader, as the decision had been made to send de Baissac elsewhere.

When Mary found out that de Baissac would not be returning, she was devastated. When fellow agent Charles Hayes witnessed her breaking down over the development, she revealed to him the truth. She suspected she was pregnant and de Baissac was the father. He had promised he would marry her but now he was gone and she had no idea what she would do.

Hayes was distraught when he heard Mary's news and attempted to help. He informed Landes of the situation, who wanted to send her back to London as soon as possible. , Mary refused. She had hidden her state for months and predicted the baby would be due in November.

Landes was troubled and unsure how to handle the situation. He eventually decided not to tell London as it came at a bad time for the network. Instead, he encouraged Mary to cut off contact with the agency and take enough money to get to a safehouse outside of Bordeaux. Meanwhile, Grandclément, disgruntled by his removal as leader of the organization, turned traitor.

He had gone to the Germans with information about the network, even showing them where the supplies from the arms drops had been carefully hidden. What followed was arrests of many members associated with the networks. Hayes was among those captured and was shot in the process. Approximately 300 Resistance members had been killed due to Grandclément's betrayal, a crushing blow to the cause.

Away from danger, Mary stayed in hiding in a nursing home in a small suburb of Bordeaux, where she had her daughter by cesarean in early December. She named the infant Claudine, most likely after the child's father. When she left the nursing home shortly after, she intentionally left no forwarding address and settled into a small apartment in Poitiers, an apartment Lise de Baissac had used at one point during her service.

A master at deception, Mary was able to create a whole new identity for herself with the money that Landes had given her. She began to seek out black market ration books and papers to support herself and her newborn. , it wasn't long before her luck ran out.

Just 2 months later, on February 18, 1944, she was awoken by the Gestapo in the early hours of morning and arrested. They believed her to be Lise de Baissac and promptly imprisoned her. Claudine was claimed and looked after by the French Social Services while Mary sat in a prison cell, determined to weave a fool-proof cover story for herself.

Mary's talents in languages are ultimately what saved her. Her fluent Arabic convinced the Germans that she was a Frenchwoman from Egypt. It also helped that she was fluent in German, gaining sympathy from her captors. Right before Easter of that year, she was released and went in search of her daughter.

The search was long and difficult. Mary was devastated at the separation but determined to find her child, she persisted. At last, she found Claudine in an orphanage. Having made many friends during her search, Mary was offered a place to stay in a small country house near Poitiers, owned by the de Vaselot family.

As the months passed by, Mary lived comfortably in the country house, awaiting news. The Allies finally landed in France in September and Bordeaux was liberated from German control. Claude and Lise de Baiassac went to France in search of Mary soon after, following her trail from Bordeaux to Poitiers. They eventually found her through an acquaintance and Claude met his daughter for the first time. Together, the four of them returned to London.

Upon returning to London, Mary and Claude were married on November 11, 1944. The marriage was apparently one of just propriety, as the couple lived separately.

Life After the War

Mary was deeply impacted by her time in the war, suffering from depression. It seemed that the horrors she'd been through had taken their toll on her. She found purpose becoming a translator and giving private French lessons. Mary lived a quiet life after the war, not giving interviews about her service and staying out of the public eye. Some time in 1960, Mary and Claude divorced, finally calling an end to their marriage of propriety.

Mary received the Croix de Guerre from the French government but, unlike her fellow SOE agents, received no awards or honors from the

United Kingdom government. It seemed that the inconspicuous Mary had slipped past their notice in the years following the war. We do know she passed away in January of 1983 at the age of 79.

An agent with a unique journey, Mary's story is one of survival. She worked hard to keep the networks operational, even when left behind by her lover in the midst of danger. Though her story was not one thought deserving of valor, her life is a testament to hope and courage. Mary has earned her spot among the remarkable women in this book.

Chapter 14:

Josephine Baker (June 3, 1906 to April 12, 1975)

Early Life

Josephine Baker was born Freda Josephine McDonald on June 3, 1906, in St. Louis, Louisiana. Her parents, Carrie McDonald and Eddie Carson were would-be entertainers. Though not married, the couple had a vaudeville song-and-dance act together. At 1 year old, Josephine got her first taste of show business when her parents incorporated her into the act, bringing her onstage with them.

Around the time Josephine was 16 months old, her mother had another child. This addition of a son to the family made Eddie realize he was not ready to settle down. He left his partner and children to continue his career, leaving Carrie in devastation. Not only was she left penniless, but she had also lost her chance at her dream.

Distraught at this development, Carrie would take it out on young Josephine. She became a harsh and demanding mother who resented Josephine for resembling her father. She worked as a wash woman to support her family but made her bitterness clear.

During her early years, the family barely scraped by, living in a low-income neighborhood near Union Station. The neighborhood mainly consisted of rooming houses, brothels, and apartments without indoor plumbing. Josephine was often dirty and hungry as a child but she developed street smarts early on.

When Josephine was 5, her mother married Arthur Martin, a kind man but one who was perpetually unemployed. After their marriage, Carrie had a son with him, as well as two daughters. The family had grown but were still struggling to get by. To help the family make ends meet, Josephine began taking in laundry for washing. At just 8 years old, she began working as a live-in domestic for white families. While working for one family, the wife burned her hand for using too much soap.

By age 12, Josephine had dropped out of school entirely and the next year she took a job as a waitress at the Old Chauffeur's Club. At the time, she lived as a street child in the slums of St. Louis, making money doing a street-corner dance. While working her waitressing job, she met Willie Wells, whom she married at the age of 13. The union didn't last and the couple divorced within a year. Following the divorce, Josephine found work in a street performance group, the Jones Family Band.

By 1921, Josephine had made her way to New York and was performing with a vaudeville troupe. That same year, she married again at the age of 15, this time to William Howard Baker. Again, the marriage didn't last. This time, it was primarily due to Josephine chasing her dreams. When her group was booked in a New York City venue, she left him behind and the two were divorced in 1925.

Her career took off upon her arrival in New York and Josephine made a name for herself in the entertainment industry. Her early acts often utilized blackface, something which her mother disapproved of. Still, it was these acts that landed Josephine a chance to tour Paris, where her career truly flourished.

Josephine left for Paris in 1925 to open Revue Nègre at the Théâtre des Champs-Élysées. Paris turned out to be her big break. She became almost instantly famous for her sensual performances. Eventually, she became the most successful American entertainer working in France. She attempted a 1936 stint in America following her Paris success but found she never attained the same fame stateside. She returned to Paris in 1937, heartbroken. Josephine married Jean Lion, a French industrialist, and became a French citizen.

Career as a Spy

At the outbreak of the war, Josephine was recruited by the Deuxième Bureau, a French intelligence agency, as an 'honorable correspondent.' She worked alongside the head of French counterintelligence in Paris, Jacques Abtey, during her time with the agency. Much like Margery Strohm, she was able to infiltrate German social circles. She brushed shoulders with the German patrons of embassies, ministries, and nightclubs, while secretly gathering information she could feed back to her superiors.

Because of her level of fame, Josephine was able to find her way into powerful inner circles that were in the know, from high-ranking Japanese officials to Vichy bureaucrats. She attended their parties and gathered important information without ever raising their suspicion. She was in the perfect position to be a mole for the Deuxième Bureau.

When the Germans invaded France, Josephine left Paris and returned to her home in the south of France. This would not be the end of her Resistance work. She housed those who wanted to help the Free French, an effort led by Charles de Gaulle, and supplied them with visas.

As an entertainer, Josephine had the perfect cover for moving around Europe, occasionally visiting neutral nations, such as Portugal. She carried information for transmission to London concerning airfields, harbors, and German concentration camps in western France. The intelligence was written on Josephine's music sheets with invisible ink to avoid detection.

In 1941, she and her posse went to the French colonies in North Africa. Though the official reason was Josephine's health, the true purpose was to continue helping the Resistance. She pinned notes with important intelligence to her underwear, counting on her fame to preclude her from strip searches.

Though Josephine was passionate about helping the cause, a health crisis would put a halt to her spying career. She had a miscarriage that left her with an infection serious enough to require a hysterectomy. The infection resulted in peritonitis and sepsis, a deadly combination. Josephine spent time in recovery but her spy career was over.

She decided to start touring to entertain European, French, and American soldiers stationed in North Africa. At the time, the Free French had no network for entertaining the troops and Josephine saw it as a role she could easily fill. Josephine and her entourage brought joy to the troops through entertainment, allowing no civilians and charging no admission to the shows. Out of the spy game, Josephine continued to serve as entertainment for the troops until the war ended.

Life After the War

After the war, Josephine became a highly decorated individual. She received many honors from the French government, including the Croix de Guerre and the Resistance Medal. She was also made Chevalier of the Légion d'honneur and received the Commemorative medal for voluntary service in Free France. Her work to better the world was not over. Josephine still had a fight in her and eventually it would take on new direction.

Following her post-war return to Paris, she took up where she had left off in her entertainment career and was welcomed back with open arms. Bolstered by recognition of her wartime heroism, Baker took on new gravitas as a performer, delving into more serious subject matter in her acts. It was received well and Josephine became one of France's preeminent performers. She toured France and for a time, the United States, to an adoring public. In 1957, she married her last husband, Jo Bouillon.

Although still living primarily in France, Josephine became involved with the Civil Rights Movement in the United States. When she arrived in New York with her husband, they were refused reservations at 36 hotels due to racial discrimination. Frustrated by this treatment, she began writing articles about segregation in the United States. She also began traveling to the South, on one occasion giving a talk on the equality of the races in France to Fisk University, a historically black college in Nashville, Tennessee.

Furthermore, Josephine steadfastly refused to perform to any segregated audiences, even when a Miami club offered her $10,000 to do so. After that particular incident, she began receiving threatening phone calls. This did not deter her and in fact just fanned the flames of her passion.

She went on to work closely with the National Association for the Advancement of Colored Peoples (NAACP), growing her reputation as a crusader. Spurred on by the NAACP's respect, she continued to make her mark in the movement. She participated in the "Free Willie McGee" rally, a protest against the prosecution of a black man for raping a white woman under dubious evidence. She became very active in the cause, writing letters and attending protests. Around this time, she divorced for the last time.

In 1963, she spoke at the March on Washington alongside the Reverend Martin Luther King Jr., as the only official woman speaker at the event. She wore her Free French uniform, decorated with her medal of the Légion d'honneur and introduced the "Negro Women for Civil Rights." After the assasination of Reverend King, she was approached by his widow, who asked her to take up his spot as leader of the movement. After some thought, Josephine turned it down, explaining her children were too young to lose their mother.

In her later years, Josephine returned to Paris to continue her entertainment career there. She was welcomed back with open arms and had a few notable performances, attended by her loyal fans. On April 8, 1975, she starred in a retrospective revue at the Bobino in Paris, meant to celebrate her 50 years in show business.

The revue was a smash hit but 4 days later Josephine was found in a coma caused by a cerebral hemorrhage. She was lying among newspapers that featured glowing reviews of her performance. She was taken to a nearby hospital and passed away on April 12, 1975, at the age of 68.

Josephine is an interesting addition to this volume. Her intelligence work contributions were brave but short lived. , she found enough fight in her to serve the cause in other ways. Her entertainment for the troops inspired other performers to do the same and her civil rights work was brave in an entirely new way. Beloved until the end, Josephine lived a full life in her 68 years.

Chapter 15:

Elizabeth Devereux-Rochester (December 20, 1917 to March 19, 1983)

Early Life

Elizabeth Devereux-Rochestern (sometimes known as Elizabeth Reynolds) was born on December 20, 1917, in New York City to parents Aimee Margaret Lathrop and Richmond Rochester Jr. She had one sister, Aimee Christine Gunning Rochester. Her father was a soldier in the First World War and upon his return, he left his family. Sometime later, Elizabeth's mother remarried, this time to Myron Reynolds, a rich American businessman.

Under a series of governesses, Elizabeth spent much of her early education in Europe. At the age of 11, she was sent to an English public school, where she excelled at sports. An active girl, she participated in various sports including golf, sailing, tennis, riding, and even hunting. At 17, she accompanied her stepfather, who admired the Germans, on a business trip to Berlin. It was there her eyes were opened to what the Nazis were doing and turned against them and their ideology.

By the 1930s, Elizabeth was living in Paris with her mother. At the outbreak of WWII, she was still there, and wanted to help in any way she could. She volunteered to be an ambulance driver for the French Red Cross. She then began working the American Hospital shortly after, engaged in vaguely anti-Nazi activities, such as taking food to POWs. She was aided in her efforts by her stepfather's close connections with the Germans.

In late 1942 when the Germans began occupying the area, Elizabeth had a close call, nearly being interned. Shaken by the experience, she decided to attempt an escape with a group of Jews who were also fleeing the area. The original destination was Britain but the group decided on Switzerland instead, as it was closer. When she arrived at the barbed wire at the Swiss frontier with other refugees after crisscrossing France, several intelligence agencies saw potential in her as something more than just an ambulance driver.

The Swiss Secret Service, the American Consulate, and the British consulate all saw value in the work Elizabeth did as a leader for the refugee group. They were particularly impressed with her successful evasion tactics, believing her to be a perfect fit for courier work.

Career as a Spy

In early 1943, Elizabeth made several forays in and out of France, usually with refugees in tow. Eventually the Maquis took her over and, upon her promise that she'd share their weaponless plight, they helped her cross the Pyrénées. She spent some time in Spain before eventually being sent to London. That year, she received the approval of the War Office and was cleared for training with the SOE.

Elizabeth's training received mixed reviews from her superiors. She was excellent in many of the activities, such as shooting, rock climbing, and sabotage. She was terrified of parachuting. Still, she was passed along and granted her first mission.

Perhaps Elizabeth would have been less fearful of parachuting had she known the harrowing trip she'd take to occupied France in a Hudson aircraft. Upon descent, the plane clipped the belfry of a church, leaving the new agent badly shaken. Despite the chaotic descent, the plane landed in a field near Lons-le-Saunier, where Elizabeth was to meet her contacts.

Her mission upon arriving in occupied France was to act as courier to Richard Heslop, as a British part of the Anglo–French mission named Cantinier, a wireless operator for American Denis Johnson, and an intelligence agent for Charles de Gaulle. Suddenly wearing many hats, Elizabeth was kept busy by her many tasks. Heslop connected with a small existing Maquis and through his means of acquiring more weapons and explosives, the network expanded quickly. Elizabeth became busier than ever, keeping up with the growth.

The network bordered on Switzerland, an area that Elizabeth had come to know well. The land was filled with high mountains and deep valleys, pine forests, and lakes. In the winter, it was bitter cold and often covered in deep snow. Elizabeth was undeterred by the rough terrain and threw herself into her work, carrying messages and supplies. She also continued to aid refugees in the area.

Elizabeth was a force to be reckoned with. She was determined, efficient, and had very little regard for her own safety while she carried out her duties. She also had a remarkable memory, usually carrying messages she had memorized verbatim. This meant she could travel without the incriminating messages on her person, making her a valuable intelligence asset. Heslop was concerned that her distinctive looks would make her stick out like a sore thumb, despite her fluency in English and German. , he believed that as long as she continued to be successful in evading the Germans, all would be well.

As the network grew and activity increased, it attracted unwanted attention from the Germans. Near their base of operations was a German airfield where troops guarded vulnerable railway stations and factories from potential sabotage. Angered by the activity of Heslop's network, the Germans sought revenge by punishing civilians in the area. In the midwinter months, 500 farmsteads in the Haute Savoie were burned to the ground in retribution.

In the early months of 1944, the Vichy authorities stepped up their efforts against the Maquis. This led to many of the air dropped supplies landing in the hands of the Germans. In February, the Vichy authorities made approximately 100 arrests. This did not slow down the enraged Maquis, who pushed back against the assault and drove the Germans out. In March, there was a massive daylight drop of around 1,000 canisters of supplies and arms that reached the Maquis, equipping them to continue the fight.

Aside from her regular tasks, Elizabeth was almost never involved with direct sabotage plots. This changed in one particular instance when she was forced to take part in the action by happenstance. A leading member of the mission was arrested beforehand and Elizabeth had to step into his shoes, training a small group of men for the excursion and setting up the necessary explosives. The plan was delayed due to snowy conditions and the risk was great. The plan went through as planned, with Elizabeth at the head.

While carrying out her regular duties within the network, she also continued to play a crucial role in escape lines. This activity, , was causing Heslop concern, not just for the safety of Elizabeth but the safety of his network. He worried that her continued escape line work would put her in danger of being captured, leaving the network vulnerable to German infiltration. He also felt that she was still far too conspicuous to make an effective agent.

Regretfully, he arranged for Elizabeth to return to London, a decision with which the SOE agreed. Heslop arranged for her to be picked up in Poitiers in late March. Arriving in Poitiers on a cold March weekend, Elizabeth went to stay with a friend at a nearby safehouse. On the night of March 20, 1944, the Gestapo came to call, arresting both Elizabeth and her friend. It was a problem, but an apparent oversight helped them in their plight.

Elizabeth and her friend were, blessedly, given slightly different treatment than other female SOE agents who had been captured.

Without interrogation, they were taken directly to Fresnes Prison, where they were allowed to share a cell. This was most likely an oversight but gave the two women an opportunity to concoct a cover story to explain Elizabeth's presence at the house. They finally decided on the story that she was a French citizen who had traveled to Switzerland to avoid internment as an American citizen. She had grown homesick and returned to Paris, selling her jewelry to do so.

Even more unusual than her initial treatment was that Elizabeth wouldn't need her cover story for a while. It wasn't until some time later that she was finally interrogated. At this point, she was living in solitary confinement, friends slipping her extra food. The interrogations continued but went fairly well, the Germans seeming to believe Elizabeth's clever lies. They never once linked her to her work with the SOE or London.

In June, the long-anticipated D-Day landings happened. Not long after, Elizabeth was tried before a judge attached to the Germany Army. She was accused of having a fake French identity card in her possession. Ironically, this was actually the only real identity card she had kept. During the trial, the name of the one who betrayed her was revealed and Elizabeth was saddened to discover it was one of her Red Cross friends. At the end of her trial, she was imprisoned in a POW camp until being liberated by American soldiers at the end of the war.

Life After the War

After the war, Elizabeth was honored by the French government with the Légion d'honneur and the Croix de Guerre. She was also recognized by the United Kingdom government with the War Medal and the 1939–1945 Star. These decorations recognized not just her bravery but her tireless effort. She was invaluable not just to the intelligence agency, but to the refugees whom she helped escape.

With her intelligence career behind her, Elizabeth lived in Paris, working in advertising. She was named in the will of Jane L. Stanford, the former California governor in the 1950s. This was due to Stanford's niece adopting Elizabeth's mother and her two daughters. Stanford University disputed the will, and a lengthy legal battle ensued. In 1957, the court sided with the heirs and Elizabeth received her inheritance. Shortly after, she received the diagnosis of multiple sclerosis. In wake of this news, she retired quietly and lived her later years in Brittany, where she stayed until her death. In 1983, she passed away at the age of 65.

Elizabeth is an unusual spy in this book. She was inconspicuous and by all accounts, did not accomplish as much career-wise as many of her peers in this book. , it is clear while looking over her life that she was a hard and dedicated worker, committed to the cause. Furthermore, she supplemented her Resistance work by assisting refugees, unwilling to abandon them. Perhaps it was because she remembered being one of them. Though she might not be as decorated as others, Elizabeth undoubtedly lived a remarkable life.

Chapter 16:

Virginia Hall (April 6, 1906 to July 8, 1982)

Early Life

Virginia Hall was born in Baltimore, Maryland on April 9, 1906, to parents Barbara Virginia Hammel and Edwin Lee Hall. The family was quite wealthy and Virginia was their youngest child. Her father was of English–Dutch descent and even owned a theater. Growing up, Virginia was more aware of English and French history than the history of her home country.

Because of her parents' affluent status, Virginia was very well educated. She first attended Roland Park Country School, before continuing her education at Radcliffe College (now part of Harvard University) and Barnard College (now part of Columbia University). In her college days, she studied French, German, and Italian and was quite a gifted linguist by the time she left. She later attended George Washington University as well, where she studied French and Economics.

Driven and ambitious, Virginia wanted to finish up her schooling in Europe. She studied in France, Germany, and Austria before securing an appointment as a Consular Service clerk at the American Embassy in Warsaw, Poland. A few months later, she transferred to Smyrna (now known as Izmir, Turkey). The ambitious Virginia was growing frustrated. She wanted to be a part of her country's Foreign Service as more than just a lowly clerk and it had yet to happen.

In addition to the professional rut she was in, Virginia had an unfortunate hunting accident in 1933 and the lower half of her left leg had to be amputated. What would have crushed many others just injected Virginia with resolve. With an artificial leg, which she had named "Cuthbert," and her trademark confidence, she learned to walk almost smoothly by lengthening her stride. By the end of 1934, she was back working as a clerk in the United States Consulate in Italy.

Over the years, Virginia made several attempts to become a diplomat with the United States Foreign Service, but at the time women were rarely hired for the role. She kept having doors shut in her face as she tried to climb her way to the top. One particular incident in 1937 involved her being rejected by the Department of State due to a rule about hiring disabled people as diplomats. The president at the time, Franklin D. Roosevelt, even wrote a letter regarding her hiring. After all, he lived with a disability as well. The letter went unheeded, and Virginia resigned in early 1939.

Career as a Spy

At the start of the war, Virginia became an ambulance driver for the Army of France. She quickly learned that she was not suited for jumping in and out of the ambulance because of her false leg. Frustrated with the job and disgusted at the 1940 Franco–German Armistice, Virginia quit and made for Britain by way of Spain, arriving at the London United States Embassy.

Over the course of the next year, she proposed her suitability for work with the SOE. She argued that she was not only fluent in French and German, but her nationality would allow her relatively free movement in France. Finally, soon-to-be "F" Section leader Maurice Buckmaster recognized the potential of these attributes and took the young aspiring agent under his wing.

Subsequently, Virginia joined the SOE in April of 1941. What followed was a crash course of training in weapons, communications, resistance activities, and security measures. She even received special training from Buckmaster himself during her time in the program. In August, she was deployed to Vichy, France, which was occupied and nominally independent at the time of her arrival.

Virginia was the second female SOE agent to be sent to France by the agency's "F" Section and the first one who stayed for an extended period. Her cover was as a journalist for the *New York Post*, giving her the ability to interview people, gather information, and file stories with details crucial to Allied war strategists. During her time gathering intelligence, she was based out of Lyons. Talented at disguises, she altered her looks to further blend in.

From her arrival in Vichy, Virginia was a pioneering agent for the SOE. This meant having to learn a lot of the necessary skills of a field agent on her own, including arranging contacts, finding suitable hiding places, and supervising the distribution of the wireless sets. She founded a network of SOE agents known by the name Heckler. Among her recruits was Germaine Guérin, who owned a prominent brothel in the city. With her connections, Guérin made several safehouses available to Virginia and passed along useful tidbits of information that had been overheard in her brothel.

Virginia was nothing if not cautious, which informs her lengthy and successful service as an SOE agent. She was an expert at avoiding capture and in October 1941, declined an invitation to a meeting of SOE agents in Marseilles, sensing danger. As it turned out, the meeting was not safe and the French police raided it, capturing 12 agents. After the event, Virginia became one of the few SOE agents still at large in France and the only one with the means to transmit communication with London. To aid the cause, American diplomat George Whittinghill allowed Virginia to smuggle reports and letters to London.

The winter of 1941 and early 1942 were a miserable experience for Virginia. She complained in a letter to London about her rough conditions and remarked that if they sent her a bar of soap, she would be "both very happy and much cleaner" (Purnell, 2020). Without access to a wireless operator, the few agents left in occupied France had only the diplomatic pouch to get messages to London.

Still, Virginia kept at it in the field, determined to aid the war effort in any way she could. She continued building contacts in southern France and even assisted in brief missions with SOE agents Peter Churchill and Benjamin Cowburn, earning high regard from them both. When agent Georges Doboudin arrived in Lyons, Virginia avoided him and refused to introduce him to her contacts, referencing his lax security. When the SOE sought to make Doboudin her superior, she told them to "lay off" (Purnell 2020).

A woman in a man's game, Virginia was often underestimated by her male superiors, but she proved to be a capable agent who cleared the way for others who came after her. She also had a tough reputation as someone who didn't suffer fools lightly. In August 1942, she met with Richard Heslop, who became suspicious, demanding to know who "Cuthbert" was. She responded by knocking her wooden foot against the table leg, producing a loud, hollow thunk. If nothing else, she had guts and a sense of humor.

Virginia took on a new task in her Resistance responsibilities as the war continued. She began helping British airmen who had been shot down or crashed over Europe, allowing them to escape and return to England. Downed airmen who found their way to Lyons were instructed to go to the American Consulate and say they were a friend of "Olivier." Olivier was actually Virginia and she, with Guérin the brothel owner's help, would hide and feed them until they were able to depart for England. She helped dozens of Allied airmen during this time.

In October of 1941, Virginia learned that 12 agents had been arrested by the French police. A wireless operator who had been imprisoned managed to get a message to Virginia, who began planning. She recruited Gaby Bloch, the wife of one of the prisoners, as an ally in her jailbreak plan. Bloch often visited the prison to bring food and other items to her husband, including tins of sardines. With tools smuggled in and the sardine tins, he was able to fashion a key to the barracks door. As Virginia was too well known to visit the prison herself, she operated in the background, assembling safehouses and helpers.

On July 15, 1942, the prisoners broke free and after avoiding a massive manhunt, all of them met up with Virginia in Lyon by August 11th. From there, she assisted in smuggling them to Spain, where they were taken back to England. Several of the escapees returned to France, leaders of their own SOE networks in the area. Virginia's determination in freeing the men led to later success for the Resistance.

, the mission wasn't over for Virginia. In the wake of the escape, the Germans were incensed and responded with force. The Gestapo flooded into Vichy with around 500 agents at their disposal. The Abwehr was also stepping up their efforts to infiltrate and disband new "F" Section networks. Virginia was in the thick of their reprisal as they focused their efforts on Lyon. She attempted to utilize her contacts within the French police but due to renewed pressure from the Germans, they were no longer reliable allies.

Virginia had to be particularly careful in the wake of this new reality. Her caution kept her uncaptured as networks folded around her. In May 1942, she agreed to have messages from the French-run Gloria Network transmitted to London. In August, the network was infiltrated and disrupted. This made Virginia especially suspicious of an alleged agent who approached her with what he claimed was valuable information. The agent in question was actually Robert Alesch, the Abwehr agent who had destroyed the Gloria Network, so her suspicions were well founded.

, he was able to convince both her and London of his legitimacy. Alesch gained access to Virginia's contacts and was able to capture several wireless operators. Consequently, the double agent was able to transmit several false messages to London in Virginia's name. Her caution was unfortunately not enough to stop this highly effective Abwehr agent. Fortunately, he would lose access to her in the coming months.

On November 7, 1942, Virginia received word from the American Consulate that an Allied invasion of North Africa was imminent. The following day, the invasion occurred and the Germans responded in kind by moving to invade Vichy. Virginia, ever cautious, correctly anticipated that this would mean suppression by the Gestapo and the Abwehr would become more severe. She decided she would leave to avoid capture in the aftermath. Without telling even her closest contacts, Virginia fled, escaping by train to Perpignan and then walked through the Pyrenees to Spain. She covered 50 miles over 2 days, deeply uncomfortable on her artificial leg.

Upon arriving in Spain, Virginia was arrested by the authorities there for crossing the border illegally. The American Embassy was able to eventually secure her release. For some time, she continued to work for the SOE in Madrid before returning to London in July of 1943, where she was made an honorary Member of the Order of the British Empire with very little fanfare.

Although she requested to be sent back as an agent, the SOE declined to do so. She was compromised, they reasoned, and therefore a security risk to send back into the field. She was determined to remain part of the agency. She took a wireless course and contacted the American Office of Strategic Services (OSS) about a job. She was hired by the Special Operations branch of the OSS at the low rank of second lieutenant and on March 21, 1944, returned to France, as she had so deeply desired.

Armed with her determination and a fake French identity card in the name of "Marcelle Montagne," Virginia went back to work arming and training the Resistance groups. They were to support the imminent Allied invasion and needed to be prepared. Their training covered sabotage and guerilla warfare, so as best to support the Allies when the time came.

During this time, Virginia had adopted an entirely new persona. She changed her appearance to appear as an old woman, hiding her signature limp with the shuffle of 'old age.' Her mission was to help set up a new network by the name of Saint. Since it was somewhat unheard of at the time for women to lead the networks, she was sent over with Henri Lassot who would head up Saint. Virginia acted as his wireless operator. Over time, she began to distance herself from Lassot because she found him to be a loud-mouthed security risk. She instructed her contacts not to give him any information on where she was.

Breaking free of Lassot, Virginia needed an ally. She knew that her accent would give her away as being American and needed someone who could speak for her when necessary. She found this ally in a French woman named Madame Rabut. With Rabut's assistance, Virginia traveled around France, committed to continuing her work. She organized drop sites, secured safehouses, and made a new network of contacts.

Virginia would next get the assignment to aid the Maquis in harassing the Germans in support of the Allied invasion of the south on horizon, part of Operation Dragoon. In July, she was sent to the Haute-Loire department. Arriving on the 14th, Virginia dispensed with her disguise and set up her base of operations in a barn near Le Chambon-sur-Lignon.

Despite her capability, she was met with resistance from the Resistance leaders. They had a hard time seeing her as an authority figure due to her gender and low rank. She told the leaders of the Maquis that she would finance them and secure arms if they would allow her to advise them. They remained frosty until she received three planeloads of supplies in late July, earning their reluctant cooperation.

With the supplies from London, Virginia and her band of Maquis Resistance fighters undertook a number of successful sabotage missions, succeeding in leaving the Germans harried. Now a part of the French Force of the Interior, they forced the German forces in their area to withdraw and head north with the rest of the retreating troops.

With the collapse of the Nazi regime in April of 1945, Virginia and several other agents made their way to Paris. It was there that Virginia wrote a letter listing those who had helped her, suggesting them for commendations before resigning from the OSS. The war had ended and she was ready to step down from her post.

Life After the War

Virginia, though often underestimated, became highly decorated after the war. She was awarded the Croix de Guerre by France and made a Member of the Order of the British Empire by the British government. She was also recognized by the United States. William Joseph Donovan personally awarded her a Distinguished Service Cross in September of 1945; it was the only one awarded to a civilian in the course of WWII. President Truman wanted the award to be a public affair, but Virginia declined the idea, stating that she was still operational and eager to continue her work, post-war.

Virginia was eager to discover the fates of those with whom she'd worked in France. Some of her closest associates had been captured and sent to concentration camps but Virginia was relieved to discover they had survived their imprisonment. She secured 80,000 francs to be sent to her associate, the brothel owner Germaine Guérin. However, many of her contacts had not survived the war.

In 1947, Virginia joined the Central Intelligence Agency (CIA), one of the first women hired by the agency. She was not to get the same type of assignment there, designated to a deskbound role of intelligence analyst. She resigned a year later, only to return in 1950 to another desk job.

In 1951, her career would get a shot of excitement. That year, she began working as a member of the Special Activities Division of the CIA. Alongside fellow agent Paul Goillot, Virginia worked supporting undercover operations to prevent the spread of Communism in Europe. The two would marry in 1957.

Despite her determination, Virginia received poor performance reports from her superiors during her time with the division. She was useless at performing the bureaucracy that the work demanded. She eventually retired at the mandatory retirement age of 66, in 1966. Virginia and Goillot retired to a farm in Barnesville, Maryland, where she lived until her passing on July 8, 1982. She was 76.

Virginia Hall is undoubtedly one of the most remarkable spies to have a career during WWII. Her fierce determination commanded respect from all who worked with her. She was a master at evading capture, always careful and suspicious. This healthy dose of paranoia kept her out of German clutches and alive. Even after the war, she kept herself in the intelligence game, unwilling to relinquish her intelligence career. Commendable until the end, Virginia has been honored by several books and a movie. People still remember her because she was an unforgettable force.

Chapter 17:

Elvira Chaudoir (1910/1911 to January 1996)

Early Life

Elvira's exact birthdate is unknown, though it is thought to be either late in 1910 or early in 1911. We know she was born into wealth. Her father was a Peruvian guano exporter and diplomat and growing up in Paris, Elvira enjoyed quite a posh lifestyle. During her upbringing, she attended a private school, becoming fluent in English, French, and Spanish.

Highly educated and openly bisexual, Elvira was an incredibly intelligent woman who grew bored of the socialite scene. Looking for excitement, she eloped with Belgian stock trader Jean Chaudoir at the age of 23. The union was short and rife with affairs. Though they didn't officially divorce, Elvira decided they no longer had anything in common and moved to Cannes with her girlfriend, Romy Gilbey, in 1938.

In Cannes, Elvira enjoyed gambling, though she often lost. She continued to gamble away her (quite rich) girlfriend's money until the Germans invaded France in 1939. Distressed by the invasion, Elvira and her girlfriend fled to England.

Upon her arrival in England, she went back to old routines and continued to lose her money gambling. While losing her girlfriend's money in cards, Elvira would often complain about the lack of interesting work available to her as a Peruvian. On one such occasion, she was overheard by an RAF officer and her name was passed around until reaching Lieutenant Colonel Claude Edward Marjoribanks Dansey, the assistant chief of MI6. What followed would be the beginning of a unique and remarkable spy career for Elvira.

Career as a Spy

Lieutenant Dansey reached out to Elvira using the pseudonym "Mr. Masefield" in 1940. The two met up and after Dansey mentioned his awareness of her financial difficulties, he managed to convince Elvira to begin working for MI6. He pointed out that due to her father's diplomatic status and her Peruvian passport, she could easily travel to France under the pretense of visiting him. Seeing a unique opportunity, Elvira had her own suggestion: letting herself be recruited by the Germans so that she could provide false information on behalf of MI6. It was a risky gamble but Dansey saw the merit in the plan and agreed to it.

Elvira was trained in the skills required for spy work and taught how to use invisible ink to send seemingly innocuous letters with hidden messages. She was given her first codename, "Cyril," and her case officers were Christopher Harmer and Hugh Astor. She was subsequently deployed to France to take on the dangerous mission that she had chosen for herself.

While in France, in the spring of 1941, Elvira was approached by an unscrupulous French collaborator by the name of Henri Chauvel. Through this connection, she made the acquaintance of Helmut Bleil, a German spy. Elvira began courting him, going out to nice restaurants with him at night. Finally, after a few dates, Bleil suggested to Elvira that she could make money providing political and industrial information about Britain to his 'friends.'

Elvira's father served as a Peruvian diplomat in England before being assigned to Vichy, France. The Abwehr were particularly interested in Elvira because they assumed she had connections to diplomatic circles, making her an invaluable source of information. Bleil gave her the codename "Dorette" and arranged for her to receive payments under the false pretenses of alimony payments. He gave her invisible ink, something he didn't know she already had training in, and instructed her to write messages that would be passed to Chauvel, who would bring them to Bleil.

Upon Elvira's return to England she reported to MI6, who passed her off to MI5 (the British domestic counterintelligence agency) for work as a double agent. When MI5 ran background checks, they were unsure of the mission's merit, due primarily to the unclear relationship Bleil had with the German government. Elvira's "lesbian tendencies" were also brough up as a cause for concern. She had a reputation as a shallow socialite with a colorful sex life, something that raised eyebrows within the agency.

Despite the objections, Elvira was added to the double-cross system team on October 28, 1942, with her brand-new codename "Bronx." As part of her cover, she was set up with a job at the BBC. She was a newly minted double-agent who had her share of doubters. Her contributions would soon silence them.

While Elvira was working as a double-agent, MI5 tapped her phone to monitor her pro-German sentiments and financial situation. As her double-cross handler instructed her, she began planting half-truths, propaganda, and fabricated statements from fake people in her letters to Chauvel. This successfully obscured any valuable information they might have gleaned from an actual spy sympathetic to their cause.

Elvira turned out to be effectively deceptive, confusing the Germans with her incomplete and falsified information. One of her letters boldly claimed that the British had made significant strides in preparing to defend against gas warfare, stockpiling large amounts of chemical weapons they would use in retaliation. The Germans trusted her completely and took her at her word when she reported to them. Her handler at the time described her as "probably one of our most reliable agents" (Macintyre, 2016).

Now a trusted 'spy' among the Germans, Elvira continued to sow discord among the Germans, while safely disguised as a sympathetic supporter. Bleil, completely in her confidence, requested that she go to the Lisbon bank and send a message indicating where and when the attack would occur.

As the Allies planned their impending invasion, they were concerned about the German forces on the western coast of France. The fear was that they would easily mobilize to reinforce the Germans at Normandy. In support of Operation Overlord, Elvira was instructed to send a coded telegram to her German 'friends' that the attack would take place in Biscay in a week's time.

Due to Elvira's misdirection, the Germans were completely unprepared for the D-Day landings. They had an entire tank division ready for the Allies in Biscay while the Allies landed in Normandy. Her infiltration and misinformation gave them the upper hand and the Allied forces were able to take the Germans almost completely by surprise. The risky gamble that Elvira had bet on had finally paid off in a significant way.

Following the D-Day landings, Elvira wrote a letter to Bleil bemoaning the misinformation, claiming it was due to her informant. The feigned shock was received well and the Germans continued to trust her, despite the disaster that the Biscay mix-up had caused.

After the initial D-Day landings, Elvira and other agents continued to send misinformation. Included among the false claims was that Normandy was just a diversion, attempting to panic the Germans and leave them scrambling. She managed to stay undetected and uncaptured until the end of the war, though her influence within German intelligence was waning. On one particular trip to Madrid, she was not able to locate a single spy and wrote them a scathing letter. Afterwards, they asked her to send a telegram about where the next strike would take place.

As the Allies took the fight to the Germans, Elvira was there to pass on intelligence that would lower their desire to resist. She began suggesting capitulation to the Nazi forces, promising that they would be treated with mercy. She cited her friends in political circles to further the legitimacy of her claims. MI5 was impressed with the strides she made and finally viewed her as a valuable agent.

The sexually adventurous gambler who had raised eyebrows at the beginning of her career had proved her worth. Her quick thinking and effective deception left the Germans open to the strategic plans of the Allies. Her contributions significantly impacted the results of the war.

Life After the War

Despite her newfound respected reputation in British intelligence, Elvira did not desire a long career in the field. Upon declaration of peace, she retired from her position within MI5, choosing a quieter life. Perhaps her taste for adventure had finally been sated. Whatever the case, she decided on a more settled life.

Her retirement took her to a small town in the south of France, using her newly inherited fortune from her father to settle down comfortably. She began running a gift shop by the name of l'Heure Bleu. Finding her life suitable, she continued doing so for the next five decades.

Elvira did her best to avoid gambling by steering clear of casinos, and even though she had inherited money, by 1995 she had run short on funds, nonetheless. Upon receiving word of this, MI5 Director General Stella Rimington arranged for a £5,000 check to be sent to Elvira with a letter that stated: "A way of making the point that her wartime service is still remembered and appreciated" (Macintyre, 2016). Though she had never been awarded honors for her service, the agency still remembered the importance of her contributions. In January of 1996, Elvira passed away at the age of 86.

Elvira has an interesting distinction in this book of being an incredible influential spy while receiving very little honor for it. She is too frequently erased from history but her story is one worth telling. An underestimated woman from the beginning, she broke through barriers and blazed a trail for those coming behind her. Her false information led to success in the single most important event of the Allies offensive strategy.

Bravery of Remarkable Women

The women in this book are a diverse cast of characters. They were born in countries all over the world. Their backgrounds spanned the socio-economic spectrum from poor laborer to celebrated socialite.

The women described here did not enter into the espionage blindly, although some did seem to stumble into it. At the time of their first missions, they were fully aware of the demands. They knew that the risk of capture would be an ever-present risk. Still, they answered the call. Some left husbands and children behind as they embarked on this War effort.

Each of these women had fascinating, complex lives outside of their role as spies. Their stories are compelling not just because they accomplished much but because at the end of the day, they were everyday people who had lives rich with love, adventure, and heartbreak.

There is a tendency to remember a person for their accomplishments, easily forgetting that there is a whole life woven throughout that exciting story. From Krystyna Skarbek, the spy who fell in love, to Elvira Chaudoir, the seemingly flighty heiress turned expert double-agent, the stories of these women go beyond historical dates. To truly appreciate their contributions, it is necessary to view them as everyday people doing exquisitely remarkable things.

All of these women faced difficult decisions, tragedy, and hardship. They carried their burden because they knew the cause was too important to abandon. It wasn't just the bravery of these spies that made them remarkable in their wartime service. It was also their hard work and indomitable spirit. Without the grit and determination - and sometimes, even elbow grease - their missions may have failed.

These women were not remarkable because of circumstance. They were remarkable because of the choices they made. We often look back over history and consider what we would have done in similar circumstances. You don't need the right circumstances or the right background to be useful when duty calls. You just need conviction.

About the Author

Arianne Cousteau is an amateur historian whose grandparents came from Europe to the United States in the late 1920s. During WWII, her father served in the US Army Air Corps. She is a retired antique furniture broker and small business owner. She has shared her business acumen to help other women launch their own businesses. Her natural curiosity about human behavior and accomplishment is what drives her interest in the role of women in all aspects of science, politics, sports, business and the arts, particularly women who have inspired others to be brave, to live life to its fullest, and to embrace the challenges of life in whatever era we find ourselves. When not visiting family in California and Europe, Cousteau splits her time between Chicago and the wilderness of northern Michigan and Canada.

List of Abbreviations

BBC	British Broadcasting Corporation
FANY	First Aid Nursing Yeomanry
MBE	Most Excellent Order of the British Empire
MI5	Security Service (United Kingdom)
MI6	Secret Intelligence Service (United Kingdom)
OSS	Office of Strategic Services
SOE	Special Operations Executive
SS	Schutzstaffel (the organization largely responsible for genocide)

References

Burack, E. (2020, April 20). *This extraordinary holocaust survivor just celebrated her 100th birthday.* Alma. https://www.heyalma.com/this-extraordinary-holocaust-survivor-just-celebrated-her-100th-birthday/

Elliott, S. (2015). *I heard my country calling: Elaine Madden, unsung heroine of the SOE.* The History Press.

Elliott, S., & Fox, J. (2011). *Children who fought hitler.* John Murray.

Escott, B. E. (2012). *The heroines of SOE : "F" Section: Britain's secret women in France.* The History Press.

Field, M. (2014, November 25). *Pippa's astonishing story recognised.* Stuff. http://www.stuff.co.nz/national/63516307/pippas-astonishing-story-recognised

Grimes, W. (2017, August 29). Jeannie Rousseau de Clarens, Valiant World War II Spy, Dies at 98. *The New York Times.* https://www.nytimes.com/2017/08/29/world/europe/jeannie-rousseau-de-clarens-dead-french-spy-in-world-war-ii.html

History.com Editors. (2018, August 21). *American women in World War II.* A&E Television Networks. https://www.history.com/topics/world-war-ii/american-women-in-world-war-ii-1

Ignatius, D. (28 December 1998). After five decades, a spy tells her tale. *The Washington Post.* https://www.washingtonpost.com/archive/politics/1998/12/28/after-five-decades-a-spy-tells-her-tale/8bfa5aae-5527-4eb5-8e45-878f1ec823fb/

Harvey, R. (2015). *Margery Booth: The spy in the eagle's nest*. Utopia Emporium.

Loftis, L. (2019). *Code name: Lise. The true story of World War II's most highly decorated spy*. Gallery Books.

Macintyre, B. (2016). *Double cross: The true story of the D-Day spies*. London Bloomsbury.

Merriam-Webster. (n.d.). *Definition of spy*. https://www.merriam-webster.com/dictionary/spy

Mulley, C. (2014). *The spy who loved: The secrets and lives of Christine Granville*. St. Martin's Griffin.

Nancy Wake. (2011, August 8). The Telegraph. https://www.telegraph.co.uk/news/obituaries/military-obituaries/special-forces-obituaries/8689765/Nancy-Wake.html

O'Connor, B. (2014). *Churchill's angels*. Amberley.

Purnell, S. (2020). *Woman of no importance: The untold story of the American spy who helped win World War II*. Penguin Books.

Stafford, D. (2017, December). *Nancy Wake obituary*. The Guardian. https://www.theguardian.com/world/2011/aug/08/nancy-wake-obituary

Starns, P. (2018). *ODETTE: World War Two's darling spy*. The History Press.

Thomas, G., & Lewis, G. (2017). *Shadow Warriors of World War II: The Daring Women of the OSS and SOE*. Chicago Review Press.

Wake, N. (1994). *The autobiography of the woman the Gestapo called the White Mouse*. Pan Australia.

Wood, E. (2002). *The Josephine Baker story*. Sanctuary.

Printed in Dunstable, United Kingdom